ROO in FAITH and JUSTICE

CHRISTIAN PERSPECTIVES
AND KEY THEMES ON PALESTINE

Edited by
REBEKAH CHOATE, KRISTA JOHNSON WEICKSEL,
AND PETER MAKARI

chalice
PRESS

Front cover photo provided by Dar al-Kalima University

Print: 9780827232310

EPUB: 9780827232327

EPDF: 9780827232334

ChalicePress.com

Contents

Foreword

Rev. Dr. LaMarco Cable and Rev. Shari Prestemon

We have the pleasure of serving as Co-Executives of Global Ministries, an innovative collaboration of the Christian Church (Disciples of Christ) and the United Church of Christ established nearly thirty years ago. Through this shared work, we walk with approximately 250 partners in nearly ninety countries in pursuit of our mission: to receive and share the good news of Jesus Christ by joining with global and local partners to work for justice, reconciliation, and peace.

Partnership is integral to all we do. It is the commitment we share as two denominations engaging in this work together. It is also the model we have deliberately chosen for our ministry with others across the world. Our global partners are churches, nonprofit organizations, and ecumenical entities firmly rooted in the local communities and countries where they reside, intimately engaged with the daily life and concerns of the people. Our relationships with these global partners are ones steeped in mutual respect and care. We learn from each other, lift prayers for one another, and grow in faith together. When our partners experience pain or injustice, we grieve with them and ensure our advocacy is guided by their wisdom and experience.

Our partnerships in Israel and Palestine are long-standing and deep. Our mission involvement in the region stretches back two centuries, and today we are actively engaged with a dozen partners in Israel and Palestine plus several more regional partners focused on Middle East concerns. The events of October 7, 2023, and all that followed in the unbearable months thereafter were thus not merely headlines for us in Global Ministries, but the grueling, lived experience of people who are our friends and the consequences of a long history with which we were already familiar. The "issues" of Israel and Palestine are for us always "enfleshed."

This book is in many ways a testament to the depth and importance of our partner relationships. While Global Ministries staff with expertise in the region and subject matter have provided here their own excellent reflections, much of the content offered in this volume is in fact written by our partners in Israel and Palestine. They are leaders of organizations and movements in Palestine. They are passionate advocates for peace with justice. They are respected thought leaders in Palestine and far beyond Palestine. They are also Palestinian Christians, essential voices in the "Holy Land" where Christianity is daily becoming a smaller presence at risk of disappearing entirely.

We need to hear what these faithful and prophetic leaders have to say to us. We need to understand what the headlines we read in our news media really mean from the perspective of those on the ground and to learn about the complexities and realities of the local situation in Palestine and Israel that will never even make it into our headlines. We need to be challenged, inspired, and moved toward action and advocacy. No doubt the voices of our partners, and the broader context and history provided in this book, will do all of that.

We invite you to read this book with full hearts and open minds. It is a powerful testimony of faith and of witness. It is also a symbol of our steadfast promise to our partners: to accompany them in trials and rejoicing and to work with them without ceasing for peace and for justice.

Introduction

Dr. Peter Makari

The years 2023–2024 have become an especially tragic marker on the historical timeline of the Middle East. Since the escalation in violence, the war Israel has waged on Gaza following the attacks perpetrated on October 7, 2023, by Hamas has resulted in Palestinians experiencing intensive bombardment; the destruction of homes, cities, and whole communities; multiple displacements; the deaths of tens of thousands of people with many more injured or unaccounted for; and widespread starvation, together amounting to ethnic cleansing. Palestinian and other Middle East partners, South Africans, and experts around the world – as well as United Church of Christ and Christian Church (Disciples of Christ) leaders - have been clear in their assertions that what is happening in Gaza is nothing less than a genocide. The physical space of Gaza has suffered what people are calling domicide (the destruction of homes and living quarters) and ecocide (the destruction of the environment). Violence extends to the West Bank as well, with settler and military attacks on Palestinians there, too. Southern Lebanon and northern Israel have been another theater of missile exchanges, and by early October 2024, Israel has expanded its military assaults to Beirut and the Beqaa Valley in Lebanon, to Yemen, Syria, and Iran.

Multiple sessions have been convened at the United Nations, both in the General Assembly, where the vast majority have urged an end to Israel's campaign, and in the Security Council, where efforts to seek a ceasefire have been stifled by countries with veto power. There, the United States has provided diplomatic cover for Israel. The U.S. has also provided Israel with massive quantities of arms and military aid and assistance during these months while cutting off support for the United Nations Relief and Works Agency (UNRWA) to provide humanitarian aid for Palestinians. UNRWA serves about six million Palestinian refugees in Gaza as well as the West Bank, Jordan, Lebanon, and Syria in areas of education and health care, as well as basic needs, and is a significant employer of Palestinian refugees. Multiple cases have been filed in the International Court of Justice (ICJ) to stanch Israel's assault. In January 2024 the ICJ found it was "plausible" that Israel has committed acts violating the Convention on the Prevention and Punishment of the Crime of Genocide. The modern international order built on international law, conventions, and principles of human rights has been exposed in its limitations and double standards, particularly as the concurrent cases of Russia-Ukraine and Israel-Palestine are set side by side.

The Israeli prevention of access to Gaza by mainstream commercial media has been somewhat offset by social media and alternative sources that offer firsthand and real-time accounts from Gaza, primarily by Palestinians who live there and are living through the campaign—and documenting it—around the clock. The period since October 7, 2023, has been revelatory for some and has motivated many to mobilize in the cause of peace and justice, seeing the struggle of Palestinians as part of a larger cause to end oppressive colonial systems and global racism. In streets and on campuses in the U.S. and around the world, hundreds of thousands of people have mobilized to support a ceasefire and to call their governments to account for providing Israel with the weapons it has used to carry out its effort.

Even so, Palestinians continue to remind us that history did not start on October 7, 2023. For Palestinians, the current tragic episode is the continuation of an injustice that spans a century and is part of an "ongoing *nakba*," or catastrophe, that began in the late 1940s when hundreds of thousands of Palestinians were displaced and dispossessed of their homes and communities. The timeline of this ongoing *nakba* includes many years and episodes across the decades, including the Middle East wars of 1948, 1956, 1967, and 1982; the *intifadas* ("shaking off") that began in 1987 and 2000; and escalations in conflict in Gaza and beyond of 2006, 2008–2009, 2012, 2014, 2021, and now 2023–2024. The visible violence of the devastating campaign in Gaza has overshadowed the structural violence throughout Palestine of more than seventy-five years. It is the daily reality of humiliation, of denial of freedom of movement and worship, of home demolitions, settlement expansion and settler violence, administrative detention, collective punishment—the constant endurance of a brutal occupation, hidden from public view, that chips away at human dignity.

The places of Israel and Palestine are dear to us as Christians—because of the biblical history centered there, because of the people (siblings in Christ, as well as Jews and Muslims), and because of the call we accept to seek justice and pursue peace. The United Church of Christ and Christian Church (Disciples of Christ) have deep connections there. The stories of our faith heritage—including the life, ministry and witness, passion, crucifixion, and resurrection of Jesus Christ—took place there. Both churches have been engaged in mission in the Middle East over the past two centuries—the first Congregational missionary went to Jerusalem in 1821 and the first Disciples missionary in 1851.

The two churches' understanding of mission has changed radically since those first encounters; today, through Global Ministries, the Disciples and UCC engage in a mission defined by the core values of presence, mutuality, community, justice, and peace. Together the Disciples and UCC have shared in ministry with Palestinian Christians for decades. Global Ministries' core values mean that we are present with, stand in solidarity with, and accompany our partners in times of celebration and challenge, as well as in the less eventful times.

Further, the Disciples and UCC are committed to justice and peace in the world. The voices of our partners in the region are central in forming our perspectives of the realities as lived by partners there. They have been critical in the development of policy resolutions considered at the UCC's General Synod and the Disciples' General Assembly over the decades, and in our churches' public witness in our own contexts in North America. Our partners have been persistent in their invitation for us to walk in solidarity with them and raise their voices in advocacy. Such perspectives are especially critical since U.S. policy in the Middle East has been an impediment to peace, justice, and the fullness of life for the people of the region. As North American churches we have a special responsibility to educate and advocate so that elected officials might also have access to the unique perspectives we do because of our partnerships.

As Global Ministries seeks to participate meaningfully in ongoing efforts to be a voice and force of decolonization in the world, in the church, and of mission, we place a high value in centering the voice of our partners in the discourse. Our partners in Palestine and Israel have consistently urged us and others to hear their cries and to participate with them in their work and witness as well as in their struggle in the cause for Palestinian rights and dignity in the face of Israeli occupation and oppression, which often go without being held to account. Their voices are authentic and legitimate. They cannot be ignored, marginalized, or negated. Jesus taught us to love our neighbor. They are our neighbors. Because they live and witness in a place far away, our churches do not always have regular access to converse with them or know them in a personal way, as we might with neighbors who are physically nearer to us. We hope, therefore, that this book might help to fill in gaps and provide partner voices and perspectives in an accessible, meaningful way.

Part of the role of Global Ministries, which is responsible for nurturing relationships with our church partners around the world, is to bring the voices of our partners to the Disciples and UCC. One way Global Ministries can do that is to offer resources for the church for education, study, and engagement. This book is an attempt to do just that.

For many the Middle East is an intimidating topic, seemingly too complicated to grasp. Yet it still fascinates, perhaps for its mixture of history, religion, politics, intrigue, and even its foreignness. Israel/ Palestine is perhaps one of the most written about subjects from the points of view of history, theology, politics, economics, and society, with much nonfiction, fiction, poetry, journals and articles, graphic novels, and other forms. Libraries are replete with volumes of such literature.

In the past three decades more and more of our partners have written and published in English conveying their perspectives and stories for a global audience. Those contributions to the literature are distinctive in that they offer a particular Christian perspective, which raises the profile of the Christian community, a numerical minority but not in any way "less" in their rootedness in Palestine and Palestinian society. Currently the Christian Palestinian community comprises a little over 1 percent of the Palestinian society in the lands of Israel/Palestine; but according to a study by the Diyar Consortium, one of our partners, Christian educational, medical, social service, and other institutions are the third highest source of employment in Palestine, following only the Palestinian Authority and the United Nations. Churches and church institutions continue to offer a witness of hope and of faith, proud of their heritage in the land that they trace back to the beginnings of Christianity.

Our aim in this small book is to offer a point of entry to voices of our partners and leading Palestinian Christians while also providing a primer on some of the key issues they face today. This volume is meant to motivate its readers to explore more deeply the issues, ideas, and people introduced here. The thematic chapters are deliberately short and digestible so readers unfamiliar with a topic can begin to consider it. We hope those who are more familiar with the issues can use this book as a guide for study in groups and congregations.

Invaluable and essential, the partner-written chapters are insightful, challenging, informative, and in some ways provocative. Because of their lived experience and daily encounter with their context, partners often use language that church members and others living far away might not have considered. Naturally, they are better able to present, contextualize, analyze, and think critically about their experience than anyone removed from the immediate context. And they are therefore farther ahead to name their realities in ways that those outside with far less intense engagement may not yet have concluded. We invite you to read with an open mind and heart.

In this volume, we are proud to gather contributions from several eminent Palestinian Christian leaders, thinkers, and theologians.

Collectively, they and their work have made important differences in Palestinian life and society and how the world—especially the global church—understands the reality. Individually, each one has earned prominence in their field. We are humbled to receive their contributions, grateful to them for offering these chapters, and proud that they lead or have led institutions in Palestine with which the Disciples and UCC have partnered. Their perspectives are rich and personal.

The thematic chapters that serve as a primer to historical and contemporary issues include a brief treatment of modern history, the genesis and reality of Palestinian displacement as refugees, political and social geography as a tool of fragmentation, colonialism and specifically settler colonialism, and the apartheid framework as it applies in Israel/Palestine. The volume offers insights and background on the topics of Christian Zionism and antisemitism that are critical in Christian circles, especially for those involved in interfaith relations. The book also traces the evolution of Disciples and UCC resolutions as approved by General Assembly and General Synod, which help guide the ways our churches advocate and seek change. Those policies include the use of economic measures to seek justice, including questioning U.S. military aid in the region, topics that are also covered. The book is organized in several sections. The first and second sections provide historical and contextual background before moving into a section on some important religious questions. The UCC and Disciples do not consider the main issue in Palestine/Israel to be religious in nature, but there are certainly religious factors that cannot be ignored. Section 4 addresses some of the current history and reality, including colonialism, settler colonialism, apartheid, and a critical aspect of U.S. involvement—military aid. Section 5 looks ahead and offers some perspectives on how the issue of justice might be addressed. Finally, as this book is being prepared in the midst of Israel's continuing assault on Gaza, a Palestinian Christian reflection on the occasion of Holy Week and Easter is an especially poignant and clear challenge to the world. The chapters are written by Global Ministries staff and by UCC and Disciples partners. As part of our effort to decolonize mission and the church, it is imperative to center the voices of partners, and this book has attempted to do just that. We are immensely grateful to our Palestinian Christian friends who have made such important contributions to this volume and to the witness and presence of the Palestinian Christian community over these many years.

We are also deeply grateful to Chalice Press and particularly to its president, Brad Lyons, who encouraged us to work on this book and provided an opportunity for these perspectives to be published under one cover.

My first visit to Palestine was with a church study delegation in January 1992, during the first *intifada*. Living in Egypt, where I have family roots, it was transformational for me to have had the chance to meet Palestinians in their homes and land and to hear about their reality in context. I remember hearing a survivor of the 1948 *Nakba* tell us her story while sitting in her home in a refugee camp in Gaza. Her passion and clarity of memory have stayed with me. I also recall holding a rubber-covered bullet that staff at the Episcopal al-Ahli Arab Hospital in Gaza collected from a patient they had treated, a victim of the Israeli army's response to Palestinian demonstrations resisting occupation. There is nothing soft about a rubber-covered bullet. I look back at the border crossing we made from Gaza to Egypt at Rafah and how empty the departure hall was. It took us a while to cross out of Gaza, then it was another ten hours by bus to Cairo. That first encounter was impactful for me, as issues of justice were so clear. I think of Rafah today, where more than one million of Gaza's 2.3 million Palestinians are displaced, and the safety that they seek. My next visit was my first trip in my capacity with Global Ministries and was during the first week of the second *intifada* in September 2000, just weeks after the infamous collapse of peace talks at Camp David. Again, this visit made an impression upon me to witness their steadfastness in the long struggle of Palestinians for justice and rights—their *sumud*.

As I continue to visit partners, often with church leaders and delegations, I have witnessed that, even as time passes, the reality on the ground worsens day by day and year by year, without resolution. Yet I see partners' commitment to create and nurture positive facts on the ground, even in the midst of occupation, and in refugee camps that have been inhabited for more than three-quarters of a century. Palestinian resistance to occupation and to injustice takes many forms, but at its most basic, carrying on with everyday life—going to school and work, shopping, marking family occasions and religious holidays, and simply entertaining hopes, dreams, and aspirations—in the midst of all kinds of unimaginable challenges is resistance, and it is life. "To exist is to resist." It is a privilege for me to help bridge cultures and contexts, and I hope that this slim volume—published in a time of especially escalated violence visited on Palestinians and heightened tensions in the region, but that addresses the longer historical context and core issues—will provide an impetus for our church members and perhaps a wider audience to consider, and re-consider, these Christian perspectives on Palestine of those rooted in faith and justice.

Section 1

Historical Background

Palestine is our homeland. We are deeply rooted here. For those Palestinians exiled around the world, Palestine lives in them. Palestine is in every corner of this earth. We will never relinquish our God-given rights of living in dignity and justice.

"Easter Amidst a Genocide," Rev. Dr. Munther Isaac

CHAPTER 1

Israel/Palestine:
A Brief Historical Overview

Rebekah Choate

Depending on who you ask, the October 7, 2023, attack by Hamas and subsequent war on Gaza have their roots in events in 2007, 1967, 1948, 1920, 1917—or since the dawn of time. What is indisputable is that the people who have lived on the land of historic Palestine have been diverse and have lived peacefully together with their neighbors—Jewish, Muslim, Christian, Druze-Arab, and non-Arab.

In 1917, as the European powers were considering how to divide the Ottoman Empire after World War I, the British government announced in the Balfour Declaration its support for the creation of a "national home for the Jewish people" in Palestine, then part of the Ottoman Empire. This was a political decision made by the British in support of the Zionist movement, which emerged in the late 1800s promoting Jewish nationalism, at least in part in response to European antisemitism. The Balfour Declaration led to an increase in support for a Jewish homeland in Palestine by Jewish communities around the world, and it was a core component of British policy in 1920 when the British Mandate for Palestine was established. The 1920s and 1930s saw increased Jewish emigration to Palestine, indirectly leading to the establishment of the State of Israel in 1948, which coincided with the end of the British Mandate in Palestine. Significantly, the text of the Balfour Declaration also includes the provision that "nothing shall be done which may prejudice the civil and religious rights of existing non-Jewish communities in Palestine." This clause is notable for its reference to—but not by name—the indigenous Palestinian people. It has generally been ignored.

2

Foreign Office,
November 2nd, 1917.

Dear Lord Rothschild,

I have much pleasure in conveying to you, on behalf of His Majesty's Government, the following declaration of sympathy with Jewish Zionist aspirations which has been submitted to, and approved by, the Cabinet

"His Majesty's Government view with favour the establishment in Palestine of a national home for the Jewish people, and will use their best endeavours to facilitate the achievement of this object, it being clearly understood that nothing shall be done which may prejudice the civil and religious rights of existing non-Jewish communities in Palestine, or the rights and political status enjoyed by Jews in any other country"

I should be grateful if you would bring this declaration to the knowledge of the Zionist Federation.

The Balfour Declaration, written by British Foreign Secretary Arthur Balfour to Lord Walter Rothschild, a prominent member of the British Jewish community, was an expression of the commitment and support of the British government for "the establishment in Palestine of a national home for the Jewish people." Palestinians still ask what right the British had to make such a promise on land that was still part of the Ottoman Empire where only a small Jewish minority lived.

Following the British announcement in 1947 that it would end its mandate by the following May, the United Nations adopted a plan of partition in November 1947; and through the establishment of the State of Israel in May 1948, the violent displacement and dispossession of the Palestinian people occurred along with the fragmentation of Palestinian society, destruction of their political rights, and dispossession of their homes, property, communities, as well as national identity and nationhood. Palestinians call this time the *Nakba*, the Arabic word for catastrophe. About 750,000 Palestinians were forcibly displaced or expelled to neighboring countries by Jewish militias and became refugees. Only about 150,000 Palestinians remained in what would become Israel. More than 400 towns and villages were destroyed or depopulated, and thousands of Palestinians were killed in dozens of documented massacres. These towns and villages were either left to decompose or were bulldozed and taken over by Jewish militias who then laid claim to them, renamed them with Hebrew names, and repopulated them with Jewish settlers.

The *Nakba* remains a traumatic event for Palestinians, both for those who lived through it and for those generations that came after. Many Palestinians also talk about the ongoing *nakba*, referring to Israel's continual occupation, violence, and injustices toward Palestinians. The fact that Palestinians were made essentially stateless by the *Nakba* has ongoing implications for the recognition of their rights and their legal status. Palestinian citizens of Israel, who make up just over one-fifth of Israel's citizenry, have different rights than those Palestinians who live in East Jerusalem, the West Bank, or Gaza, who in turn have different rights than Palestinian refugees in Syria, Jordan, and Lebanon.

For those Palestinians who remained on the land that became the State of Israel in 1948, their rights were immediately curtailed as they lived under martial law until 1966. Palestinian refugees who attempted to return to their homes during this time were killed or otherwise prevented from entering the newly established Israel. Palestinians also continued to be expelled and towns and villages destroyed along with some documented massacres during this period.

In the 1967 War, Israel occupied East Jerusalem, the West Bank, the Golan Heights, and Gaza and the Sinai Peninsula, which had been controlled by Jordan, Syria, and Egypt, respectively. This war led to another wave of displacement, with many Palestinians fleeing to Jordan, some made refugees for a second time. This occupation of the West Bank, including East Jerusalem, and Gaza continues today. Israel annexed the Golan Heights in 1981, and that was recognized by the U.S. in 2019, although negotiations for its partial return continued. Israel returned the Sinai to Egypt following the Camp David Accords and the Israeli-Egyptian Peace Treaty of 1978 and 1979. Palestinians living in the West Bank are still living under military law and governed by military courts and institutions.

Administrative detention is a legal tool used by the Israeli military to detain Palestinians in jails indefinitely without the rights and protections of Israeli civil law. Rights would include knowing the charges against oneself, having access to legal counsel, and a trial in a civil court.

Ever since the creation of the State of Israel, Palestinians have been fighting for their human, civil, and political rights. Palestinian refugees have been fighting for their rights as refugees. Palestinians living under occupation in the West Bank, East Jerusalem, and Gaza have long sought their rights as an occupied people in a variety of ways: at the United Nations, with the United States government, within the Israeli government and military systems, through civil disobedience, and through protests. Palestinian resistance has employed nonviolent and occasional violent means. Of these, the first (1987–1993) and second (2000–2005) *intifada*s (Arabic for "shaking off") are the best known.

Palestinian citizens of Israel also have struggled for their rights as a numerical non-Jewish minority group within Israel since 1948. Their rights were further suppressed with the Israeli Knesset's adoption of the 2018 Israel Nation State Law, which states that "the right to exercise national self-determination" in Israel is "unique to the Jewish people" and thus essentially enshrines two separate classes of citizens, establishes Hebrew as Israel's official language and downgrades Arabic to a "special status," and establishes "Jewish settlement as a national value" and mandates that the state "will labor to encourage and promote its establishment and development," which creates a legal right to exclude non-Jews from living in Jewish communities.

DISCUSSION QUESTIONS

1. Does any of this historical context help you to better understand the current reality? Why or why not?

2. Is any of this information new to you? Is any of it different from things you've learned before or read or heard in the news? If yes, how does it feel to receive this information?

3. The *Nakba* was a painful part of Palestinian history that continues to shape current realities in the region. Are there events in the history of your country that continue to shape current realities in your context?

CHAPTER 2

Gaza: A Background

Dr. Peter Makari

*Then an angel of the Lord said to Philip, "Get up and go toward
the south to the road that goes down from Jerusalem to Gaza."
(This is a wilderness road.)*

Acts 8:26 (NRSVUE)

Gaza today is a strip of land twenty-five miles long and four to
six miles wide, where 2.3 million Palestinians live; among them, fewer
than one thousand are Christian. Three-quarters of the population
are refugees or descendants of those displaced in 1948 from towns,
villages, and cities near Gaza. It is one of the most densely populated
spaces on earth—at least as dense as New York City, the most densely
populated city in the United States.

Gaza's history spans four centuries. It has been an important
crossroads for trade given its location on the Mediterranean coast at
the intersection of Africa and Asia. It is mentioned in the Bible in the
story in Acts 8 of Philip and the Ethiopian eunuch. Christianity in
Gaza traces its roots back to the late fourth century CE and the efforts
of St. Porphyrius. Gaza came under Islamic control in 637 CE. Over
the centuries it has been controlled by the Romans, different Islamic
rulers, the Crusaders, the Ottomans, Egypt, and now Israel.

Gaza was supposed to be part of Palestinian state according to the
1947 UN partition plan defined by UN General Assembly Resolution
181 on November 29, 1947, following the British decision to end its
mandatory control of Palestine. The partition plan allocated 55 percent
of the land for a Jewish state and 43 percent for a Palestinian Arab
state, and the remainder—primarily in Jerusalem and Bethlehem—was

to be under international custodianship owing to the presence of sites sacred to the people of the three faiths: Judaism, Christianity, and Islam. That proposed partition was rejected by the Arab states (and others) because it was perceived to have been imposed from outside without regard for the claims, presence, and views of the indigenous Palestinian people. Following the declaration of the establishment of the State of Israel in May 1948 and the Palestinian experience of *Nakba*, approximately two hundred thousand of the 750,000 Palestinians who were displaced sought refuge in Gaza.

Before 1948 the Gaza Strip did not exist as such—it was open and accessible with no border separating it from the rest of historic Palestine. When armistice lines were drawn at the end of the 1948–49 war, the Gaza Strip was created as a separate entity and was under Egyptian administration until 1967. The refugees who had fled to Gaza were still very close to their original homes, towns, and villages and did not accept the idea of separation by a border.

In November 1956, during the Suez Crisis—known in the Arab world as the Tripartite Aggression—in which England, France, and Israel attacked Egypt over access to the Suez Canal that Egyptian President Gamal Abdel Nasser had nationalized weeks before, the Israeli military killed hundreds of Palestinians in the Khan Younis refugee camp, imposed a curfew, and occupied Gaza until March 1957.

Israel's current control of Gaza resulted from the 1967 War, when Israel also occupied the West Bank and East Jerusalem, the Golan Heights, and the whole of the Sinai Peninsula, taking Gaza and the Sinai from Egypt. While the Sinai was returned to Egypt as part of the Camp David Accords (1978) and peace treaty signed between Egypt and Israel (1979), Gaza remained under Israeli occupation. That occupation allowed for some freer access by Palestinians in Gaza to Israel for work, especially in the earlier years.

In 1987 the deaths of four Palestinians in Gaza, killed by an Israeli truck driver in a collision, sparked the first *intifada* (Arabic, "shaking off," also referred to as "uprising"). Three of the four Palestinians were from one of the eight refugee camps in Gaza. The Islamic Resistance

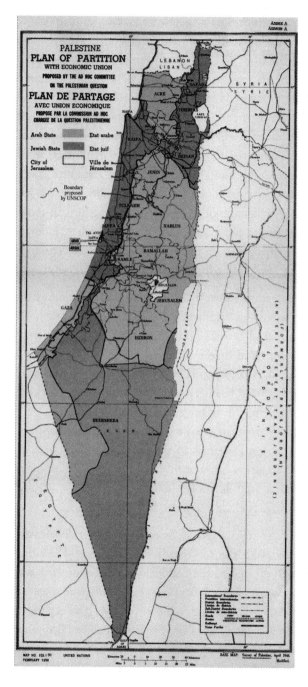

United Nations Resolution 181 of November 29, 1947, called for the partition of the land of Palestine so that 56% would form a Jewish state, 43% an Arab Palestinian state, and 1% would be an internationally-controlled area that included Jerusalem, Bethlehem, and surrounding areas due to their religious importance to Jews, Christians, and Muslims. The Partition Plan was not realized as Palestinians and other Arab governments rejected the premise, and the new State of Israel controlled 78% of the land following the 1948 war.

Movement, in Arabic known by its acronym Hamas (also an Arabic word that means "zeal" or "enthusiasm"), formed during the *intifada* to resist Israeli occupation and was tacitly supported by Israel as a counterweight to the more secular Palestinian Liberation Organization (PLO). As an Islamic group, Hamas traces its ideological roots to the Egyptian Muslim Brotherhood. It has called for the establishment of an Islamic state on historic Palestine but has tacitly accepted the idea of a Palestinian state along the 1967 borders for more than fifteen years. Hamas continues to support and implement armed resistance. Since its election and ascension to control in Gaza in 2006–2007, it has maintained three distinct components: a political wing (it is an active political party in Palestine and so functions as such, which includes its political office and apparatus); a military wing, as an armed resistance unit; and a provider of social, educational, and cultural services.

Gaza has remained occupied by Israel since 1967, during which Israel established twenty-one settlements, illegal under international law. The nine thousand settlers who lived there eventually were removed in 2005 as part of Israel's "disengagement" plan. Following Palestinian elections in 2006, when Hamas took control of Gaza, Israel sealed it off. Since 2007 it has been under a heavy Israeli blockade with limited access for people to leave or enter, constraints on access to fishing in the Mediterranean, and little access for food and supplies, including reconstruction materials. In the years since, the blockade has vastly affected the economic and health situation of Palestinians living there. Gaza has been described as an "open-air prison," sealed off with a border barricade and surveilled by Israeli drones.

Even before October 7, 2023, Gaza's economy depended heavily on foreign aid. In 2015 the UN predicted Gaza could become uninhabitable by 2020 due to the blockade, a prediction that was largely accurate before October 7, 2023, and certainly true since. In 2016 prominent Harvard academic Sara Roy published an expanded version of her landmark study, "The Gaza Strip: The Political Economy of De-development," arguing that since 1948 Gaza has gone from an economically integrated and connected territory to one that has been deliberately isolated from the West Bank and from Israel, resulting in its de-development, which she characterized as intentional.

Israel has waged military operations in Gaza in 2006 (Operation Summer Rains), 2008–2009 (Operation Cast Lead), 2012 (Operation Pillar of Defense), 2014 (Operation Protective Edge), and 2021 (Operation Guardian of the Walls) in response to the kidnapping of an Israeli soldier, rocket attacks, and other acts by Hamas, which has cited its resistance to Israeli occupation and blockade, Israel's imprisonment of thousands of Palestinians, and Israel's violations of sacred spaces of worship such as al-Aqsa Mosque in Jerusalem as its motivation. All of those military operations—which Israel has termed "mowing the grass"—have destroyed residences and infrastructure and killed and injured thousands of Palestinians in Gaza.

In March 2018 Palestinians in Gaza began regular Friday demonstrations dubbed the Great March of Return, calling for the right of return for Palestinian refugees to be respected, based on UN Resolution 194 (1948). These peaceful demonstrations lasted for over a year, until December 2019. They were met with live fire from Israeli soldiers, shooting from outside of Gaza, killing more than two hundred Palestinians over this time.

When Hamas launched thousands of rockets and killed and captured hundreds of Israelis on October 7, 2023, Israel responded by waging war on Gaza, which has continued to this writing. This war has resulted in tens of thousands of Palestinian deaths and many more injured, 90 percent of the Palestinians of Gaza displaced from their homes and communities multiple times, and almost all of the people there facing starvation.

Even though it is small in numbers, the Christian community in Gaza has offered an important witness there for decades. Among our partners, the Middle East Council of Churches' Department of Service to Palestinian Refugees has offered vocational training, medical clinics, and psychosocial counseling for Gazan Palestinians since it was established following the *Nakba*. Al-Ahli Arab Hospital is a diaconal service of the Episcopal Diocese of Jerusalem. Al-Ahli Hospital is Gaza's oldest hospital, founded in 1882 by the Anglican Church Mission Society. From the 1950s to the early 1980s it was owned and operated by a Baptist mission and was known as the Baptist Hospital, until it was transferred to the Episcopal Diocese, which continues to operate it today. Dar al-Kalima University, a Christian university serving the whole Palestinian society, is dedicated to teaching arts and culture. Its main campus is in Bethlehem and has a branch campus in Gaza that was destroyed in 2024. The historic St. Porphyrius Greek Orthodox Church has served as a shelter for Gazan Palestinians during the current war on Gaza.

DISCUSSION QUESTIONS

1. Does any of this historical context about Gaza help you understand the current war? Why or why not?

2. Is any of this information new to you? Is any of it different from things you've learned before? If yes, how does it feel to receive this information?

3. Dr. Roy's study describes the intentional de-development of Gaza. What do you think the role of the church and other aid organizations should be in response to intentional de-development?

Section 2

Contextual Background

In this land, even God is a victim of oppression, death, the war machine, and colonialism. He suffers with the people of this land, sharing the same fate with them. "My God, my God, why have you forsaken me?" It is a cry that has resonated for years in this land.

"Easter Amidst a Genocide," Rev. Dr. Munther Isaac

CHAPTER 3

Refugees and the Right of Return

Rebekah Choate

Now after they had left, an angel of the Lord appeared to Joseph in a dream and said, "Get up, take the child and his mother, and flee to Egypt, and remain there until I tell you, for Herod is about to search for the child, to destroy him." Then Joseph got up, took the child and his mother by night, and went to Egypt and remained there until the death of Herod.

Matthew 2:13–15 (NRSVUE)

A Palestinian refugee under the United Nations Relief and Works Agency's (UNRWA) mandate was defined in 1952 by the United Nations as any person whose "normal place of residence was Palestine during the period 1 June 1946 to 15 May 1948 and who lost both home and means of livelihood as a result of the 1948 conflict." Under international law, the children of refugees and their descendants are also considered refugees until a lasting solution is found. This principle applies to all refugees.

In the late 1940s the UN General Assembly established two different UN refugee agencies—UNRWA in December 1949 and the UN Office of the High Commissioner for Refugees in December 1950—to respond to distinct refugee crises.

In 2023 there were six million registered Palestinian refugees under UNWRA's mandate. The total number of Palestinian refugees, however, is closer to eight million. When UNWRA was created it served about 750,000 Palestinian refugees. Those refugees have since passed their refugee status down to their children, grandchildren, and even great-grandchildren, consistent with how displaced people across generations are classified everywhere.

Even before UNRWA was established, what is now the Department of Service to Palestinian Refugees (DSPR) of the Middle East Council of Churches (MECC) was formed in 1948. A longtime UCC and Disciples partner, DSPR began as an ecumenical service organization with both international and local clergy and laity to tend to the trauma of Palestinian refugees.

Its five area committees have provided services in Galilee, Jerusalem, and the West Bank, Gaza, Jordan, and Lebanon, ever since. Work is coordinated through a central office in East Jerusalem. DSPR was an early manifestation of modern ecumenism in the Middle East, becoming a semi-autonomous unit of the MECC when it was established in 1974.

DSPR aims to enable people to organize their lives better so they can live with dignity despite the various difficulties and constraints that seek to inhibit them from "normal" living. Over seventy thousand Palestinians benefit from the health clinics in DSPR areas of operation, particularly in Gaza and Jordan. DSPR also provides vocational training, medical and psychosocial services, and education. It also has constructed cisterns in the many communities with few or no dependable water sources.

There are many international declarations, resolutions, compacts, and laws relating to refugees generally and to refugees of specific conflicts.

In the Universal Declaration of Human Rights, Article 13 states: "Everyone has the right to freedom of movement and residence within the borders of each state. Everyone has the right to leave any country, including his own, and to return to his country."

The 1951 Convention Relating to the Status of Refugees provides the internationally recognized definition of a refugee and outlines the legal protection, rights, and assistance a refugee is entitled to receive. Its cornerstone is the principle of non-refoulement, which means refugees should not be returned to a country where they face serious threats to their life or freedom.

United Nations General Assembly Resolution 194, passed in December 1948, resolves: "[Palestinian] refugees wishing to return to their homes and live at peace with their neighbours should be permitted to do so at the earliest practicable date, and that compensation should be paid for the property of those choosing not to return and for loss of or damage to property which, under principles of international law or equity, should be made good by the Governments or authorities responsible."

Despite these declarations, conventions, and resolutions, the government of Israel has refused to allow Palestinian refugees to return to their homes. That is why UNWRA continues to provide services like education, health, relief and social services, microfinance, and emergency assistance programs to all Palestinian refugees in Gaza, the West Bank, East Jerusalem, Lebanon, Jordan, and Syria. Many of UNWRA's staff are themselves Palestinian refugees, and UNWRA is among the largest employers of Palestinians.

Of the six million registered Palestinian refugees, more than 1.5 million live in fifty-eight recognized refugee camps in Jordan, Lebanon, Syria, Gaza, the West Bank, and East Jerusalem. Since October 7, 2023, the refugee camps in Gaza and the West Bank have been targets for the Israeli military. Raids into refugee camps were common before October 7 and have escalated since. Refugee camps are densely populated and often lack access to basic infrastructure. What started as temporary tent cities are now small areas that have overcrowded, deteriorating multi-story buildings with high concentrations of people living in poverty.

Of the 2.3 million Palestinians in Gaza, about 1.7 million were registered refugees from towns and villages beyond Gaza's current boundary. Therefore, most of those who are now displaced in Gaza have been displaced for at least a second time. As of mid-July 2024, just under two hundred UNWRA staff members in Gaza have been killed since October 7, the largest number of UN staff fatalities during a conflict in its history, and UN schools as well as other facilities have been targeted as well.

Israel has consistently denied Palestinian refugees their right to return to their homes and land. In contrast, Jews from other countries are encouraged to migrate to Israel and are given special priority in receiving permanent residence status or citizenship upon arrival, called *aliyah*. Since 1948 around 3.4 million Jews have immigrated to Israel. According to The Jewish Agency for Israel, 76,261 immigrated in 2022 alone, the highest number in a single year since 1999. The total Jewish population, including settlers, is around 7.4 million out of a total Israeli population of about 9.9 million. Ironically, Jewish emigration from Israel has also been exceptionally high in recent years.

DISCUSSION QUESTIONS

1. Why do you think the Israeli government treats Jewish migrants to Israel differently than Palestinian refugees who were forced to leave their homes in the area that became Israel?

2. UNRWA's funding has been cut drastically by the international community, and as an organization it has been targeted by the Israeli government for decades. Why do you think this has happened, and what do you think might happen if UNRWA becomes unable to keep serving Palestinian refugees?

3. Can you imagine being forced from your home and still being unable to return more than seventy years later? What might be lost for you and your descendants in the time of displacement?

CHAPTER 4

Attempted Fragmentation of Palestinian Society

Rebekah Choate

Now I appeal to you, brothers and sisters, by the name of our Lord Jesus Christ, that all of you be in agreement and that there be no divisions among you but that you be knit together in the same mind and the same purpose.

1 Corinthians 1:10 (NRSVUE)

Life on the ground for Palestinians largely depends on the ID card and residency of each individual Palestinian. Those living in Israel as Israeli citizens (about 2.1 million people) have the most rights as they are citizens of Israel, although their rights are not as full as those of a Jewish Israeli citizen. They have the right to vote in Israeli elections; can access municipal services such as education and health care; and may travel to Jerusalem, the West Bank, Gaza, and other countries. However, if they want to marry someone without Israeli citizenship who has a different type of Palestinian ID or status, they face significant barriers. They also face restrictions on where they are permitted to live. Some cities and towns in Israel allow only Jews to live there. Palestinian-majority towns and cities are often overcrowded, as the Israeli government doesn't grant many building permits in these areas. Arab-majority municipal budgets are lower, Arabic is no longer an official language even though 20 percent of the population is Palestinian, and public services are poor, especially when compared to the services received by Jewish Israelis.

Palestinians who live in East Jerusalem (about 361,000 people) have a Jerusalem residency card, not Israeli citizenship or Palestinian citizenship, although they are allowed to apply for Israeli citizenship, a long and difficult process. They are citizens of no country, only residents of East Jerusalem. They are permitted to travel within Israel and to the West Bank and other countries. They must follow a strict residency requirement to keep their Jerusalem residency card. If they fail to prove to the Israeli government that their main residence and center of life is in Jerusalem, they are at risk of losing their residency status. Jewish Israeli settlers have used the Israeli legal system to take Palestinian homes in East Jerusalem and the Palestinian population there frequently faces harassment from these settlers. They can vote in municipal elections but not national elections and have no representation in the Knesset (Israeli Parliament).

Palestinians who live in the West Bank (about 3.3 million people) are subject to Israeli occupation and military rule and as such, face daily obstacles to the full enjoyment of their lives. Roadblocks, checkpoints, denial of work permits, denial of travel permits, invasive searches of their cars and person, denial of home and building permits, periodic military raids, forced removal from their homes and villages, settlement encroachment, and settler violence are some of the daily traumas and humiliations Palestinians face. Most Palestinians who live in the West Bank are not allowed to travel to Jerusalem or into Israel without a permit, very few of which are granted. They also face harassment from Israeli border guards when crossing into or returning from Jordan. Their lives are characterized by a "matrix of control," Israeli-American anthropologist Jeff Halper's description of reality of the Israeli military occupation.[1]

Palestinians in Gaza (about 2.3 million people) have been living under Israeli occupation since 1967 and a strict blockade since 2007.

---

[1] Jeff Halper, "The Key to Peace: Dismantling the Matrix of Control," Israeli Committee Against House Demolitions, https://icahd.org/get-the-facts/matrix-control/

Building materials, medicine, fuel, and other "dual use" items have not been allowed to be brought into Gaza. As such, Gaza's economy has been left to rot. Most Gazan Palestinians depend on foreign aid to some extent to survive. Before October 7, 2023, very limited numbers of travel, medical, educational, and work permits into Israel or East Jerusalem were granted. Even permits to travel to East Jerusalem for medical treatment were rarely granted. The crossing into Egypt from Gaza was also tightly restricted by the Egyptian government as they coordinate that border crossing closely with the Israeli government. Gaza has been referred to as an "open-air prison" since the Israeli blockade began.

About six million Palestinians are registered as refugees with United Nations Relief and Works Agency. Many live in refugee camps in Gaza, the West Bank, Jordan, Syria, and Lebanon since they were forced from their homes and communities during the *Nakba* in 1948. They have not been accorded the right to return to their homes in Israel or compensated for their losses as laid out in UN General Assembly Resolution 194, and their descendants are also classified as refugees. Depending on where they live, refugees have different rights. Many of those who fled to Jordan were offered and accepted full Jordanian citizenship, and, in fact, about half of Jordan's population is Palestinian. Palestinian refugees in Syria have many of the rights of Syrian citizens, including the right to work and access to social services provided by the government of Syria like health care and education, but they cannot become citizens except in rare circumstances. Palestinian refugees in Lebanon have more restrictions, including what jobs they can and cannot hold.

Palestinians who live in the diaspora often have become naturalized in their new country. However, the Israeli government controls access to visit any family they have living under its occupation and disregards their foreign nationality when they arrive for a visit. So a Palestinian-American may be restricted by the Israeli government from entering Israel, the West Bank, Gaza, or East Jerusalem.

In a 2012 TED Talk Palestinian-American businessman Sam Bahour shared his family's story of fragmentation and control:

My name is Sam Bahour. I was born and raised in Youngstown, Ohio. Today I live in my father's birthplace of El-Bireh, eight miles north of Jerusalem, deep in the West Bank. Our home was my grandfather's home, too. It was also the home of his grandfathers. ... My father left Palestine for the United States ten years before the 1967 War. Therefore, he was not counted in the census that Israel took when it first seized control [of the West Bank]. Palestinians who were present received an Israeli-issued identification card giving them permanent residency in their ancestral homes. To this day my seventy-one-year-old West Bank-born father can return to his birthplace only as a U.S. tourist and for a maximum of three months. ... Meanwhile, a Jewish person born in Brooklyn, Bolivia, or Bulgaria has the full right to be a full citizen the moment he or she lands in Israel. As an American I entered Israel/Palestine the same way as my father, as a temporary tourist. Lack of permanent residency meant that I had to leave and re-enter every few months to renew my visa. That outrage continued for a decade and a half. My wife and I were never sure whether to buy a new car or not. Buy a new home or not. Pay the girls' full tuition or not. One cannot build a future on three-month planning horizons. Our occupiers know this very well. In 2006, during a visa renewal trip to Jordan, I was given after a six-hour wait a tourist visa. This time, however, my U.S. passport had handwritten in it in Hebrew, Arabic, and English "last permit." I joined the campaign for the right to enter. I also reached out to many Israeli friends to make my case for permanent residency. The Israeli military finally conceded in 2009. Or did they? As a U.S. citizen who travelled freely for 15 years, I was now classified as a Palestinian. More so than my father who was born here. That meant my Israeli-issued ID card cost me my freedom. Today I can visit Jerusalem only after getting an Israeli military permit and only then after traveling on foot through a humiliating checkpoint resembling a cattle chute. Still, I am one of the lucky ones.

The 1993 Oslo I Accord established the Palestinian National Authority (PA), which was granted limited self-governance of certain parts of the West Bank and Gaza Strip. The 1995 Oslo II Accord divided the West Bank into three administrative divisions: Areas A, B, and C. Area A is administered by the PA, which has full civil and security control and is a noncontiguous territory with about 18 percent of the total land of the West Bank. Area B is administered by both the PA and Israel, with the PA having civil control and joint PA-Israel security control and is a noncontiguous territory with about 22 percent of the total land. Area C is administered solely by Israel, which retains full civil and security control and is a contiguous territory that is about 61 percent of the total land.

The government of Israel essentially controls all access to land, water, and other natural resources despite theoretical full Palestinian governance over Area A. In actuality, the Israeli military frequently raids Area A without cooperating with Palestinian security services. Often the Israeli government takes Palestinian land, sometimes designating it a nature preserve that Palestinians are then not permitted to live or build on. Israeli checkpoints, barricades, and the separation wall all limit access by Palestinians to the land they own and use for crops, grazing, or other agricultural activities. Israeli settlers often uproot and/or set fire to groves of olive trees to drive the owners off the land so the settlement can expand.

The aquifers across the whole of Israel/Palestine are under Israeli control, meaning that settlers in the West Bank can water their lawns and fill their swimming pools while Palestinians in the neighboring town face water restrictions and shortages. West Bank aquifers are on the Israeli side of the wall despite being in occupied Palestinian areas. About 92 percent of Palestinians in the West Bank must store water in containers on their rooftops with irregular delivery to replenish these limited supplies. On average, Palestinians in the West Bank have access to about eighty liters of water per person per day. The World Health Organization's standard is one hundred liters.

In Gaza the situation is even more dire. In this current war, people in Gaza have been surviving on less than three liters of water

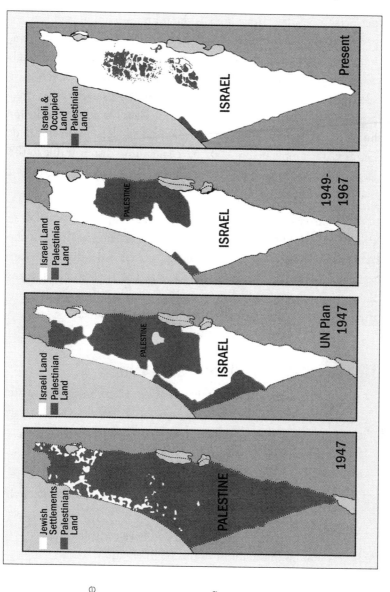

Palestinian Loss of Land (1947–present): Over the past three-quarters of a century, the physical area Palestinians have lived on and had access to has diminished. These four panels illustrate the increased Jewish and Israeli control.

per person per day. Three liters is the minimum amount of water a person needs to drink to avoid health problems related to dehydration, including organ damage and failure. This means there isn't enough water for people to clean themselves, their living quarters, and their cooking implements or for them to consume to stay healthy. Even prior to this current crisis, 97 percent of Gaza's water was unfit for human consumption. Desalination plants that helped supply much of Gaza's water supply before 2007 have fallen into disrepair due to the Israeli blockade imposed since 2007. Repair and other construction materials are heavily restricted.

Despite Israel's attempt to fragment the Palestinian population—Palestinian citizens of Israel, residents of Jerusalem, residents of the West Bank, those in Gaza, and refugees, as well as the diaspora—the sense of national unity and cohesion has not been diminished as families and communities have members in each of these groups, and the struggle for justice for all Palestinians has continued.

DISCUSSION QUESTIONS

1. Why do you think the Israeli government has attempted to fragment Palestinian society?

2. What do you think has caused Palestinians to maintain a sense of national unity?

3. Imagine you were a Palestinian-Canadian and desperately wanted to visit your favorite aunt in Gaza but were denied access. How would you feel?

4. What prayer or hope would you have for Palestinian siblings in the midst of this fragmentation?

CHAPTER 5

The Impact of the Israeli Occupation and Displacement on Palestinian Women and Their Journey for Justice

Dr. Mira Rizeq

Note from the author: Parts of this article are extracted from previous writings and presentations done internally when I worked at the YWCA of Palestine. The description and analysis provided in this article are based on my personal experience and reflections, stories and witnesses of colleagues, stories I heard from older generations in my family and in society at large.

The situation and role of Palestinian women in Palestine are largely linked with the history of Palestine since 1948 and the different phases that the Palestinians have lived through. Throughout that history and since then, human rights violations and the extent of violence of the Israeli occupation have never let up. On the contrary, Israel has been tightening its control on the whole population, making life almost unlivable. Despite this, Palestinian civil society, including women, "walked" through the different stages using different resistance, resilience, and survival strategies to stay alive and to keep its historic legacy alive.

In 1948 over five hundred villages were demolished and 750,000 Palestinians were expelled from their homes to become the first batch of refugees through forced eviction. Israel, with the help of the British Mandate, captured 78 percent of the Palestinian historic land and established the Israeli state on this land, soon to become recognized by the United States. Another war was fought between Israel and the Arab States in 1967, which resulted in the occupation of the West Bank and Gaza by Israel and which led to more Palestinians displaced or evicted to other neighboring Arab states like Jordan, Syria, and Lebanon. Today 71 percent of the total Palestinian population globally are refugees, which amounts to almost 11.5 million, displaced from other parts of Palestine that has been occupied gradually by Israel. Almost six million Palestinians live in the diaspora and are unable to return to their homes with the continued denial by Israel of their right of return and the continued failure of all peace negotiations, including the famous Oslo Accords I and II (1993 and 1994) to recognize the rights of these Palestinians, including their right to self-determination.[2]

Since its establishment in 1948, Israel has been confiscating both public and private Palestinian land, as well as agricultural land and farms; controlling water resources; demolishing homes and expelling families from their homes, shelters and safe spaces; and exacerbating the already fragile and deteriorating social, economic, and health conditions of Palestinian families and the Palestinian civil society at large. Over the years volumes of research and documentaries developed by formal research institutions, individuals, and UN reports have validated and documented all these practices.

All borders and entrances to the West Bank and Israel are controlled by Israel. As a matter of fact, Gaza has been under total siege for almost twenty years. Palestinians there essentially live in a large open prison.

To control Palestinians further under the guise of "security," Israel began building the Separation Barrier, or Apartheid Wall, throughout the West Bank and East Jerusalem, in 2002. The Wall annexed more land to Israel, separating Palestinian families and prohibiting farmers from accessing their agricultural fields, their main source of livelihood. All these controls and practices have led thousands of Palestinians to lose more of their land, homes, and livelihood. According to the Palestinian Bureau of Statistics, estimates of unemployment rates were expected to exceed 28 percent (13.1 percent in the West Bank and 45.3 percent in Gaza). Poverty levels in early 2024 were also

---

[2] 1 Demographic Statistics from PASSIA Agenda 2022.

projected to increase by 45.3 percent, rising from 26.7 percent to 38.8 percent, expected to rise further if the war, aggression, and closures of Palestinian territories continue.[3]

No UN resolution pertaining to Palestine issued since 1948 has ever been implemented, and furthermore, the international community has complacently allowed Israel to continue its grave violations of human rights with no accountability, legitimizing its policies and practices of ethnic cleansing and racial discrimination.

Hamas' stated goal in the attack on Israel it initiated on October 7, 2023, was to break the iron siege in pursuit of a just peace and to bring back the nearly forgotten issue of Palestine to the forefront of news. In retaliation, Israel has been conducting a "plausible" genocide in Gaza, according to the International Court of Justice. At this writing, almost forty thousand people—75 percent of whom are women and children—have been killed and over eighty thousand injured, in addition to several thousand Palestinians who are buried under the rubble. If the bombing and shelling and the closure of borders, including denial of passage of food and health aid, continue, these numbers will continue to rise exponentially. Israel has been using hunger as a strategy for collective punishment against the Palestinians.

Overall, the continued violence and violations of basic human rights inflicted by Israel have created a disastrous economic, social, and political situation, affecting the mental and psychological well-being of the whole population. The mere survival and resilience of Palestinians has succeeded due to the strong social fabric of its civil society.

In this reality, the Israeli occupation and its practices have affected women in every aspect of their lives and in very special ways. The Israeli occupation has certainly not been gender-blind.

On the political level, women in occupied Palestine face arbitrary arrests and aggression on a daily basis. They also suffer from a constant

---

[3] Palestinian Bureau of Statistics Highlights Socio-Economic Indicators on the Impact of the Israeli Occupation War on Gaza Strip 2023. 16 October 2023. https://www.pcbs.gov.ps/site/512/default.aspx?tabID=512&lang=en&ItemID=460 6&mid=3171&wversion=Staging

state of exclusion, fear, aggression, violence (both physical and mental), persecution, political atrocities, and constant trauma as an outcome of all the above-mentioned military practices. In the day-to-day experience of women crossing checkpoints, trying to go through special gates constructed as entry points to Jerusalem, passing through the Wall, and as they move from cities to rural areas even within the West Bank, they are reminded of the constant colonial militarization. Several research projects carried out on Palestinian women have demonstrated that women's mobility has been severely restricted because women are afraid to cross checkpoints due to physical aggression toward them by soldiers and humiliation at borders and checkpoints. Tens of women have given birth at checkpoints due to the delay of ambulances, and several others have lost their babies during delivery due to the delays in accessing health services at checkpoints.

The segregation of Palestinian land has taken its toll on the social and cultural fabric of Palestinian society. Many families have been separated by the Wall or checkpoints, keeping women isolated from their extended families, in many cases their only source of social and psychological support. Women have suffered constant loss of family members, especially activists killed by Israeli soldiers, expelled, or imprisoned. Women have had to stand strong and support their families when shattered due to home demolitions and displacement. Despite the constant efforts of the Israeli occupation to crush the social and communal fabric, women have been key in sustaining the family and the community by joining women's movements, cooperatives, and other forms of collectives that also became their main source of emotional, social, and economic support.

Since 1948 Palestinian women have always engaged in all types of community work, mostly on a voluntary basis conducting emergency response operations. These have since progressed to become more effective popular resistance contributing effectively to the survival of their families and communities. In the early 1960s and as the Palestinian political parties were forming as part of the Palestinian Liberation Organization, established in 1964, women eventually organized themselves in parallel structures to these parties, with clear political and social agendas, offering spaces for women to engage in the process of liberation. Later, women also became more active through women's committees and grassroots organizations in their localities as well as at national level. The nongovernmental sector in Palestine, which is one of the largest and strongest in the Arab world, has succeeded in supporting communities and especially women in surviving by offering safe spaces, economic opportunities, and support systems, especially in the absence of an empowered Palestinian government, for many decades.

Over the years the Union of Palestinian Women, the National Coalition for the Implementation of United Nations Security Council Resolution 1325 on women, peace, and security, and the "*Muntada*" (Coalition of Civil Society Institutions Combating Violence Against Women) have become important platforms and mechanisms for mobilizing women around political issues and national liberation. Palestine is one of the few countries around the world that have prepared and issued a National Action Plan for UN Security Council Resolution 1325, which was launched in 2014 at a national conference organized and led by the YWCA of Palestine in partnership with several women's organizations.

During the first *intifada* ("shaking off"), which began in 1987, women's participation in nonviolent resistance became more apparent and effective. Palestinian women challenged checkpoints, where they fought with the soldiers when denied crossing, despite the physical violence and aggression they experienced. Thousands of women have been detained and imprisoned over the years since 1967 and faced extreme physical violence. Despite this, women's commitment to and participation in the national liberation struggle was strengthened as a counter strategy for increased violence by the military occupation.

In 1993 the Oslo Accords were signed between Israel and the Palestinians, establishing the Palestinian Authority. The agreements later failed due to noncompliance by Israel. Right after the Oslo peace agreement, the whole Palestinian society's resilience and resistance was weakened, as many Palestinians at the time believed Oslo would bring them a lasting peace settlement based on justice. This distanced civil society and women temporarily from organized political activism, assuming and believing at the time that the Palestinian Authority would rescue civil society. With the failure of the Palestinian Authority to address the aspirations of the Palestinians for a just peace, grassroots activism and resistance gained more momentum and more legitimacy, especially amongst women, who saw their participation in the national liberation process as key and inevitable.

During the second *intifada*, which started in 2000, women's grassroots resistance was perceived as diminishing. Women's political engagement, whether through grassroots resistance or formal government structures and peace processes, have always stood out despite their oscillation, especially when compared to other neighboring countries in the Arab world.

As the economic situation worsened in the West Bank and Gaza, it was the women who suffered the consequences most. Women not only had to become the "shock absorbers" and supporters of their respective families, but they also had to find ways to contribute to family income. Several nongovernment organizations and civil society organizations intensified their support for women's economic empowerment programs as a strategy for family survival.

In the economic sphere, women continue to be severely challenged. Despite the increasing numbers and competitive abilities of female university graduates, job opportunities continue to be scarce and therefore biased in favor of male graduates, who are seen as "the breadwinners" within the predominantly patriarchal system in Palestinian society.

In light of the fact that formal labor markets have continued to discriminate against women, women have actively participated in the informal economy, through cooperatives and household economic ventures, as an alternative economic development strategy. This has never been the ideal alternative strategy because this sector continues to be largely abusive and not regulated by any laws or regulations that can protect women. Although this situation of inequity is changing, the process is slow and cumbersome. Today an increasing number of female university graduates are working in all formal sectors as school and university educators, government officials, lawyers, judges, and doctors and in other fields.

Over the years, and as political violence against Palestinians has increased, and due to the deteriorating economic situation and increasing unemployment, Palestinian society has witnessed increasing incidences of gender-based violence in their own communities and within their households, including intimate family violence, exploitation, and physical/sexual assaults by family members. Forced early marriages have increased as an outcome of the impoverishment of families, as have school dropouts, especially among young girls. Many young women have dropped out of school due to mobility restrictions and checkpoints.

In conclusion, there is nothing under the sun that Palestinian women have not witnessed and suffered from. The latest genocide in Gaza that started on October 7, 2023, has added severely to the extreme suffering and emotional load on women. The women who stayed alive through all these wars and aggressions—and the latest genocide—have to care for and protect their hungry and starving family members and children while being harassed, bombed, and forced to flee. Women have also had to watch their children being killed during the shelling and bombing and die of hunger as the siege of Gaza continues. For the women in Gaza, staying alive is both a blessing and a curse that can never be forgotten.

There may be no better way to describe the condition of women than as one Palestinian woman expressed herself. In a study conducted by Dr. Nadera Kevorkian in March 2010, commissioned by the YWCA of Palestine, one woman interviewed said:

> I have no passport, I exist nowhere, the world does not recognize my nationality, I am unable to travel or move freely, wherever I go I need a permit or travel document from the Occupying Forces, I have no health insurance, if I get sick I cannot even afford to go to hospital, I am separated from

my family through the Separation Wall, I wish I will die, and when I do, no one will miss me, we are like insects, human insects.[4]

DISCUSSION QUESTIONS

1. Women's groups and informal networks have helped Palestinian women to be resilient. Where do you see these groups and networks in your community? What is their role?

2. Do you see any similarities between the struggles faced by Palestinian women and women in your community?

3. Dr. Rizek asserts that "the occupation has certainly not been gender-blind." What do you think this means? What do you think this might look like?

---

[4] Nadera Kevorkian, "Military Occupation, Trauma and the Violence of Exclusion—Trapped Bodies and Lives," YWCA of Palestine. March 2010

Section 3

Religious Background

Because we have faith—we do not live in despair. Faith is the only thing they cannot take away from us.

"Easter Amidst a Genocide," Rev. Dr. Munther Isaac

CHAPTER 6

Christian Zionism

Derek Duncan

When an alien resides with you in your land, you shall not oppress the alien. The alien who resides with you shall be to you as the native-born among you; you shall love the alien as yourself, for you were aliens in the land of Egypt: I am the Lord your God.

Leviticus 19:33–34 (NRSVUE)

Christian Zionism is a theological and social movement that views history as the unfolding of biblical prophecy in which Israel plays a central role. Frequently it means a Christian firmly supports the modern State of Israel. But Christian Zionism has more concrete historical origins and more specific religious and political implications regarding Israel and the role of Jews and Christians in carrying forth biblical prophecy.

Christian Zionism developed out of nineteenth- and twentieth-century Protestant fundamentalism. Fundamentalists claim to read the Bible literally. Although there may be agreement on certain core beliefs, or fundamentals, other conclusions about what fundamentalist groups claim the Bible literally says often vary. Some fundamentalists read the Bible to gain a religious understanding of historical and current events and to predict future events related to the second coming of Christ. Dispensations are the eras of human history that unfold according to God's plan.

Christian Zionism is related to pre-millennial dispensationalism, which believes Jesus' return to earth to reign for a thousand years must entail the restoration of Israel's biblical glory. Christian Zionists read the Bible literally to forecast a divinely willed plan for the end of history that includes, among other events, the return of all diaspora Jews to Jerusalem to reconstitute the biblical nation of Israel. This ingathering of Jews is a condition for the rapture of Christians into heaven, a time of war and hardship called tribulation, and the return of Christ that sets the stage for a dramatic scenario of heavenly reign that ends with humanity's final judgment.

The creation of the State of Israel in 1948 confirmed for many believers that scriptural revelation was playing out as predicted in their particular view of the end times. Christian Zionists believe the founding of Israel in the "Holy Land" is a fulfillment of God's special covenant with Abraham and his descendants. Influenced by certain texts, such as Ezekiel 37–38, Christian Zionists purport to hasten the second coming of Christ by supporting Israeli policies that provide for the ingathering of Jews into the biblical lands of Israel, often referred to as Judea and Samaria, in order to prepare for the battle that would precede Christ's second coming. Christian Zionists will often support organizations committed to Jewish immigration to Israel and rebuilding of the Jewish temple in order to facilitate these apocalyptic events.

The movement has gained significant political strength in recent decades as its adherents, mainly among conservative U.S. evangelicals, have successfully supported a foreign policy based on American exceptionalism and triumphalism—the idea that the United States inhabits a special and unique place in the world and in history, ordained by God with particular responsibilities in the community of nations—and unwavering support for the State of Israel. The increased influence of Christian Zionists in U.S. society among religious leaders and politicians has strengthened America's "special relationship" with Israel and helped ensure U.S. military and financial patronage. Despite Christian Zionists' appropriation of Israel as part of Christian prophesy, the fervent support of Christian Zionists has been courted by Israeli and Jewish leaders.

Christian Zionism is based upon a literal reading of scripture, primarily the Old Testament/Hebrew Bible. Its focus is on the covenant between God and the Israelites, promising them the land, and the marking in history of different eras, inferred from scripture. The assertions Christian Zionism makes contain significant flaws in scriptural interpretation. At a most basic level, the covenant between God and Abraham offers land to the Israelites—"And I will give to you, and to your offspring after you, the land where you are now alien, all the land of Canaan, for a perpetual holding; and I will be their God" (Genesis 17:8)—but it also requires that the Israelites treat their neighbor kindly—"When a foreigner resides among you in your land, do not mistreat them. The foreigner residing among you must be treated as your native-born. Love them as yourself, for you were foreigners in Egypt. I am the Lord your God" (Leviticus 19:33–34).

Christian Zionist efforts to support charities and policies dedicated to protecting and privileging Jews in the State of Israel now cynically obscure a negative theological judgment of and prospect for Jews in the future and therefore can be regarded as antisemitic. At one level such ideological support for Israel fails to mention that the Jews who are to be gathered there would perish in the final battle if they do not convert to Christianity (see 1 Thessalonians 4–5). Equally cynical are Israelis who welcome support from Christian Zionists who do not ultimately desire the well-being of Jews.

While Christian Zionism has a particular theological and scriptural grounding, the political implications of Christian Zionism and its impact on the life of Palestinian Christians living under Israeli occupation are significant regardless of whether Christian Zionists are theologically self-aware. In his 2023 book *Decolonizing Palestine*, Rev. Dr. Mitri Raheb suggests Christian Zionism is even more expansive, including any Christians who uncritically support Israel, guided by their faith.[5]

Beyond that, and on a deeper level, Christian Zionism denies the loving and merciful nature of God for all of God's creation, as it is selective in limiting who enjoys God's favor. Christian Zionists also ignore or deny the presence and faithful witness of the Christian

[5] Raheb, Mitri. *Decolonizing Palestine: The Land, the People, the Bible.* Orbis Books, 2023.

communities of the Middle East, particularly Palestinian Christians whose heritage and sustained presence traces back to the first century CE. From Algeria to Iran and from Turkey to Sudan, there are roughly fifteen million Christians in an otherwise predominantly Muslim region. The Christians of the Middle East are part and parcel of their social, political, and economic milieu. They speak the language (Arabic, Persian, or Turkish) of their nations and are culturally indistinguishable from their non-Christian compatriots. While the Christian community in Israel/Palestine has become numerically smaller in recent decades, those who remain are steadfast in their faith.

In 2006 the Latin Catholic and Syriac Orthodox Patriarchs and the Anglican and Lutheran Bishops in Jerusalem issued a statement called "The Jerusalem Declaration on Christian Zionism." In it, they stated:

> The Christian Zionist Program provides a worldview where the Gospel is identified with the ideology of empire, colonialism, and militarism. .... We categorically reject Christian Zionist doctrines as false teaching that corrupts the biblical message of love, justice, and reconciliation. ... With urgency we warn that Christian Zionism and its alliances are justifying colonization, apartheid, and empire-building. God demands that justice be done.[6]

The desire of Palestinian Christians is for a just, peaceful, and nonviolent resolution, for an end to Israeli occupation of Palestinian lands and control over Palestinian lives, and for the respect of human and legal rights and democratic self-determination for all. They support and encourage U.S. policy that would achieve a fair and just solution.

Christian Zionist pressure on U.S. policy hinders U.S. diplomacy and interests in pursuing a just and durable peace. As an ideology that dishonors scripture's greatest admonition to love the neighbor and protect creation, Christian Zionism diminishes Christian relations with Jews around the world and especially in the Middle East. Perhaps

---

[6] "The Jerusalem Declaration on Christian Zionism," https://hcef.org/1694-the-jerusalem-declaration-on-christian-zionism/, August 29, 2006

most troubling, Christian Zionism's anticipation of a final, total war centered in the Middle East invites a perpetuation of conflict in the region and rejects any hope for human reconciliation.

The tragically un-Christian implication of Christian Zionist ideology and its effects on world affairs require that its tenets be refuted and an alternative theology of possibility and promise for all people in the Middle East be articulated, even as we pursue a faithful vision for just peace in the Middle East.

DISCUSSION QUESTIONS

1. Where have you seen Christian Zionism manifest itself in your church, your community, or your country?

2. The Bible can be read in many ways depending on cultural context, theological lens, and current ethics and norms, including the scriptures used to prop up Christian Zionism. What is a piece of scripture of which you have personally changed your reading and view?

3. What would life in Israel/Palestine look like if Genesis 17:8 and Leviticus 19:33–34 were equally obeyed?

4. Rev. Dr. Mitri Raheb suggests that Christian Zionism includes any Christians who uncritically support Israel, guided by their faith. What do you think of this expanded definition?

CHAPTER 7

Palestinian Christians

Dr. Bernard Sabella

Palestinian Christians are small in number, making up fifty thousand of the population of 4.5 million in the occupied Palestinian territories.[7] With the rich kaleidoscopic nature of Palestine and its historic Christianity, Arab Palestinian Christians—a majority of Christians in both the occupied Palestinian territories and in Israel, 160,000 to 170,000 in total—have always been part of the social, cultural, and national-political contexts of their Palestinian society. Living in and around the places that have seen the birth, life, crucifixion, and resurrection of Jesus Christ, their ties to the land center around their faith as they adhere to traditions, rites, and rituals they have inherited from their forebears. Their affinity to their people and land grew as they shared the same history and experienced the flora and fauna of the Holy Land similarly to other compatriots. Farmers, fishermen, educators, professionals in various fields, and devoted clergy, they have continued to advocate and to narrate the woes and aspirations of their people throughout the century-long turbulent times of clashes and conflict between Zionism and the Arab Palestinian national movement.

Thirteen Officially Recognized Churches

There are thirteen churches in Palestine officially recognized by the governing authorities in Palestine, Israel, and Jordan. The

---

[7] For a centennial overview of the Palestinian Christian population between the 1920s and 2020s, see Bernard Sabella's "Palestinian Christians Centennial Historical & Demographic Developments," accepted for publication in Villanova University's Journal of South Asian and Middle Eastern Studies, Villanova, Pennsylvania.

major theological distinction among the churches is that of the Chalcedonian/non-Chalcedonian division. The Council of Chalcedon in 451 attended by 520 bishops espoused the Chalcedonian Creed or Confession, which affirms Jesus Christ's two natures (divine and human), that Christ is "the same perfect in Godhead and also perfect in manhood".[8] The Greek Orthodox, Roman Catholic, and Protestant churches adhere to the Chalcedonian Creed. The Oriental Orthodox Churches—Armenian, Syriac, Coptic, and Ethiopian—believe in the single nature of Christ and do not subscribe to the Chalcedonian Creed.

The Greek Orthodox Church, comprised mostly of Arab congregants and Hellenic clergy, counts some twenty-four thousand faithful or close to 48 percent of the Christian population of fifty thousand in Palestine (i.e., East Jerusalem, West Bank, and Gaza Strip). In contrast, the Greek Orthodox within Israel number some forty thousand or some 36.4 percent of the total Arab Christian population of 110,000.

The Latin or Roman Catholic Church has a following of roughly 17,500 members, or 35 percent, in Palestine. Within Israel, the Roman Catholics are one of the smaller communities with some fourteen thousand followers or 12.7 percent of the Christian population. Of note is the role of the Franciscan Custody of the Holy Land which, since the thirteenth century, has been custodian of the holy places and of the Catholic parishioners in the Holy Land until mid-nineteenth century when the Holy See appointed a patriarch to head the Catholic Church in Palestine.

The Greek Melkite Church in Palestine has some six thousand followers, or roughly 5.6 percent of the entire Christian population; whereas in Israel, this church has some fifty-six thousand followers, or 51 percent of the Christian population. This makes it the largest church in the Holy Land comprising Palestine and Israel.

The Evangelical Lutheran and the Episcopal Anglican churches had their beginnings in the middle of the nineteenth century with the

---

[8] https://www.ccel.org/creeds/chalcedonian-creed.html

arrival of German and English Protestant missionaries. Presently both churches have Arab Palestinian presiding bishops and archbishops. In Palestine both churches have a following of close to two thousand and some three thousand in Israel, most of whom are Palestinian Arabs.

The Armenian Orthodox Church is a relatively small church with some one thousand Armenians living in the Palestinian Territory and some three thousand within Israel. The Armenians, like other Christians, keep the faith of the forefathers and persevere despite difficult circumstances.

The Syriac Orthodox Church, which uses Aramaic, the language spoken by Jesus, in its rites is home to some 1,500 followers, mostly found in Jerusalem and Bethlehem. They pride themselves that some of their families trace their roots to the early church of Jerusalem.

The Armenian Catholic, Syriac Catholic, and Maronite Churches are Uniate churches associated with Rome with relative autonomy in their rites and church matters, concentrated mostly in Jerusalem where they have their church hierarchies. All together, they number at some one thousand faithful.

The Coptic and Ethiopian churches are Oriental Orthodox and, like the Armenian Orthodox Church, believe in the one nature of Christ and hence are labelled as non-Chalcedonian. Despite the low numbers of their followers, they have had a rich history in Jerusalem, particularly in and around the Church of the Holy Sepulchre.

The rich traditions, rites, and rituals of the faithful and clergy in the different churches attest to the one faith in Jesus Christ and his mission of salvation. Christians in the Holy Land are more aware of their unity than of theological distinctions, particularly as the mounting challenges of the land call on them to witness as living stones.

Christian Population Distribution

Palestinian Christians are estimated to be close to one million worldwide today, including third and fourth generations of early emigrants, and make up close to 8 percent of the thirteen million Palestinians worldwide. All together Palestinian Christians in Palestine and Israel make up less than 17 percent of the entire Palestinian Christian population worldwide. The vast majority of the Palestinian Christian population moved abroad during different waves of emigration. Palestinian Christian emigration from the Bethlehem and Ramallah areas started toward the end of the nineteenth and the early twentieth century. A major wave of Christian emigration was from the Bethlehem area to South and Central America. In 1948 close to sixty thousand Palestinian Christians became refugees during the first Arab-Israeli war, among three-quarters of a million Palestinians. Many of the Christian refugees eventually migrated to the Americas and some to Australia, where the Christian Palestinian community in Sydney originally from Jerusalem is larger than the present Christian Palestinian community in Jerusalem itself.[9]

The Christian population in Palestine is concentrated in the central areas of the West Bank with twenty-three thousand in Bethlehem, Beit Jala, and Beit Sahour, followed by the towns of Ramallah and Birzeit and the surrounding villages of Jifna, Aboud, and Ein Arik with ten thousand and Jerusalem and its environs with 8,500, all together making up 92 percent of the entire Christian population. In the northern part of the West Bank, the town of Zababdeh with an overall population of 5,000 is home to some 3,500 Christians belonging to the Roman Catholic, Greek Orthodox, Anglican, and Greek Melkite churches. Palestinian Christians, particularly those coming from villages and farming communities, have been known as educators and professionals who have served their society well.

The Gaza Predicament

The Gaza Strip, with its 141 square miles and its over 2.3 million inhabitants, was home to one thousand Christians before October 7, 2023. With the ongoing raging war on Gaza, there is real

---

[9] Bernard Sabella's "Palestinian Christians Centennial Historical & Demographic Developments," accepted for publication in Villanova University's Journal of South Asian and Middle Eastern Studies, Villanova, Pennsylvania.

fear that the Christian community there will dwindle further. The destruction of church-run schools, bombardment of the Episcopal al-Ahli Arab hospital and clinics, devastation of training and social and cultural centers and even church buildings could spell an end to a Gazan Christian community that had survived the vicissitudes of war, calamity, and turbulent history. As of this writing, close to eight hundred Christians in Gaza have found shelter during the current merciless war in the Greek Orthodox and the Roman Catholic churches. Harrowing stories of illness, hunger, killings, injuries, and despair come out of these churches as Christians, like other Palestinians, suffer from the effects of the prolonged military conflict. Scores of Gazan Christians have succeeded in getting out of the war-torn Gaza Strip because they hold foreign passports that enabled them to leave. At one point in the history of Christianity, Gaza City claimed to be the first Christian city in the world and a Gaza school of Christian theology developed there in the early era of Christianity.[10]

An Urbanite, Well Educated, and Engaged Community

Palestinian Christians are an urban community, as well over 80 percent of them live in cities and towns. With the spread of foreign missionary schools in Palestine starting with the mid-nineteenth century, Christian children were the first to profit. Education has always been a great value not only to Christian families but to the entire population. In fact, two of the eight universities in Palestine have been founded or run by Palestinian Christians, and Bethlehem University was founded by the Holy See at the behest of local Palestinian Christians. With their education and urban background, Palestinian Christians are found in the liberal professions with an impressive percentage of nongovernmental and human rights organizations. Politically, Palestinian Christians are at ease with secular-leaning

[10] Palestinian Central Bureau of Statistics, 2017 Population Survey, https://www.pcbs.gov.ps/Downloads/book2364.pdf.

For the beginning and brief history of Christianity in the Gaza Strip up to modern times, see *Encyclopedia of Christianity in the Global South*, ed. Mark A. Lamport, Rowman & Littlefield (Lanham, Boulder, New York, London: 2018).

political factions that tend to call for a society based on the equality of rights of all citizens. Christians tend to be weary of confessionalism and prefer the pan-Arab and Palestinian identity over narrow religious identification.

According to a recent survey of Christian organizations operating in Palestine, there are 296 organizations including ninety-three schools, universities, and vocational centers; nineteen health care facilities; forty-seven social protection institutions; seventy-seven cultural and tourism centers; thirty-eight youth and scout centers; one environmental center, and twenty-one local and international development agencies that deliver a variety of services to hundreds of thousands of Palestinians. Of note are the four specialized hospitals in Jerusalem run by churches that serve a population of 330,000 patients. Services include pediatric kidney dialysis, pediatric cancer services, complicated cardiac operations, specialist maternal health, eye care, blood bank, and other sophisticated services for people with disabilities.[11]

Palestinian Contextual Theology

The development of a Palestinian contextual theology should be viewed as part of the indigenization of the local church that started in the 1970s. The installation of Palestinian Protestant bishops and the eventual elevation of Father Michel Sabbah to the Latin (Roman) Catholic Patriarchal seat heralded the way for the development of theological and contextual reflections and publications by Palestinian pastors, priests, and laity.[12] Organizations and religious persons

---

[11] George Akroush, CNEWA – Pontifical Mission and Dar al-Kalima University, "Mapping of Christian Organizations in Palestine: Social and Economic Impact," Diyar Publisher, 2021, https://www.daralkalima.edu.ps/uploads/files/Mapping%20of%20Christian%20Organizations%204Final.pdf.

[12] Bishop Najib A. Cubain was appointed in 1958 as the first Arab Bishop of the Episcopal Church in Jerusalem and the Middle East see https://j-diocese.org/wordpress/anglican-bishops/. Bishop Daoud Haddad was elected by the Synod of the Evangelical Lutheran Church as first Arab Bishop in 1979; see http://actpalestineforum.org/about/members/evangelical-lutheran-church-in-jordan-the-holy-land/. Patriarch Michel Sabbah of the Roman Catholic Church was the first Palestinian Arab in five centuries to be elevated in 1987 to the post of Latin Patriarch; see https://www.lpj.org/curia/patriarch-michel-sabbah.html.

engaged in such reflections span the different churches. In the Catholic Church the late Geries Khoury founded Al Liqa' Center with the support of Melkite Greek Catholic Bishop Lutfi Lahham. The Catholic Justice and Peace Commission was initiated by the Catholic Church in Jerusalem during the 1980s and 1990s, reflecting on the situation of the land and its conflicting turmoil. Contextual theology took a leap forward with the publication by Canon Naim Ateek of *Justice and Only Justice: A Palestinian Theology of Liberation* in 1989. The book countered the biblical arguments used mostly by Christian Zionism and highlighted calls for justice for the oppressed and disinherited Palestinians on biblical grounds and commandments. Soon after the publication of the book, the Sabeel Ecumenical Liberation Theology was founded.[13] Sabeel organized yearly international conferences to raise awareness among Sabeel Friends, mostly in North America and Europe, of the realities of Israeli occupation and the injustices committed against Palestinians.

Mitri Raheb, a Lutheran pastor in Bethlehem, published in 1995 *I am a Palestinian Christian: God and Politics in the Holy Land*. He has established two distinctive institutions in Bethlehem—Dar an-Nadwa and Dar al-Kalima University—to cater to the population of Bethlehem and Palestine. Raheb has expressed the pain experienced by Palestinians during the Israeli occupation of Bethlehem and the Church of Nativity siege between April and May 2002 with his emotive book published in 2004, *Bethlehem Besieged: Stories of Hope in Times of Trouble*. In January 2014 Raheb published the impressive *Faith in the Face of Empire: The Bible Through Palestinian Eyes*.

Issued in December 2009, the Kairos Palestine Document "A Moment of Truth: A Word of Faith, Hope, and Love from the Heart of Palestinian Suffering" addressed the issue of continued Israeli occupation and reached out to Muslims, Jews, the Israeli occupation authorities, and global public opinion to sensitize them to the "sin of occupation" and the fact that the evil was occupation itself and not the

---

[13] For the variety of activities undertaken by the Sabeel Ecumenical Liberation Theology Center, see its website: https://sabeel.org/.

people enforcing it. It was a message of nonviolence out of Palestinian Christian witness and compassion, and it spelled out the human and other costs of a continuing occupation to both the occupier and the occupied. Beside Patriarch Michel Sabbah, some of the other authors of Kairos Palestine were Rifat Kassis, the convener of Kairos Palestine; Archbishop Atallah Hanna; Revs. Mitri Raheb and Naim Ateek; and Yusef Daher, the director the Jerusalem Inter-Church Center. Recently, in December 2021, the Kairos message was reemphasized in a national meeting of Bethlehem-area Christians headed by Patriarch Emeritus Michel Sabbah to discuss the affinities and shared lives of Palestinian Christians with the larger society.[14]

In 2010 Bethlehem Bible College, which is associated with Palestinian evangelical Christians, launched its first biennial Christ at the Checkpoint conference attended by evangelicals from the United States and the Holy Land. According to the conference website, "the mission of 'Christ at the Checkpoint' is to challenge Evangelicals to take responsibility for helping resolve the conflict in Israel/Palestine by engaging with the teaching of Jesus on the Kingdom of God." To achieve this, it is necessary to "discuss the realities of the injustices in the Palestinian territories and create awareness of the obstacles to reconciliation and peace." Targeting evangelicals whose biblically-based support for Israel is not sensitive to the injustices suffered by Palestinians constitutes outreach to a key group that has blindly supported Israel and its policies, settlement activities, and punitive measures against Palestinians.[15]

In December 2021, the Patriarchs and Heads of Local Churches of Jerusalem issued a statement warning of the threats faced by Christians and churches from radical Jewish fringe groups. The statement also called for the protection of Jerusalem's distinct and historic quarters and preservation of the cultural integrity of the Christian Quarter similar to the legal protection given to the Jewish

---

[14] For the Kairos document and news of events and activities, see www.kairospalestine.ps.

[15] For more details on the Christ at the Checkpoint conference, see https://christatthecheckpoint.bethbc.edu/.

Quarter in the Old City of Jerusalem.[16] There is increasing worry among Palestinian Christians of suspicious sale deals which seek to turn over key church properties in Jerusalem to extremist Jewish groups with the tacit support and approval of the Israeli government. Of late the phenomenon of spitting on Christian clergy with desecration of churches, cemeteries, and Christian religious symbols by zealot Jewish religious groups contributes to a growing feeling of unease by laity and church leaders alike.

Palestinian Christians face the same challenges as their Muslim compatriots. Even so, and as their numbers diminish, they remain steadfast—proud of their two-millennia history and presence, committed to serving their society, and determined in the struggle for justice.

DISCUSSION QUESTIONS

1. Dr. Sabella states that Palestinian Christians are more aware of their oneness than their theological divisions. Do you think that is true in other countries where Christians are minorities? Do you think that is true in the United States or Canada?

2. According to Dr. Sabella, the first wave of Palestinian Christian migration started at the end of the nineteenth century when Palestine was still under the jurisdiction of the Ottoman Empire. Why do you think the vast majority of Palestinian Christians have moved abroad?

3. Dr. Sabella mentioned that the indigenization of the local church started in the 1970s, which allowed for the development of a Palestinian contextual theology. Why do

---

[16] "Anglican Archbishop, Other Heads of Churches and Patriarchs Issue Statement on the Current Threat Holy Land Christians Face, *Episcopal News Service,* December 14, 2021, https://www.episcopalnewsservice.org/2021/12/14/anglican-archbishop-other-heads-of-churches-and-patriarchs-issue-statement-on-the-current-threat-holy-land-christians-face/.

you think it's important for there to be Palestinian church leaders and a Palestinian contextual theology?

CHAPTER 8

Palestinian Liberation Theology

Rev. Dr. Naim Ateek

Palestinian Liberation Theology emerged around the end of the 1980s with the publication of my book *Justice, and Only Justice, a Palestinian Theology of Liberation*. Several factors contributed to its emergence.

1. The 1948 Nakba

The Palestinian people experienced the greatest shock of their life at the loss of their homeland at the hands of the western Jewish Zionist militias. This happened at the end of the British Mandate of Palestine and the beginning of the establishment of the State of Israel, when approximately three-quarters of a million Palestinians, both Christians and Muslims, fled in fright or were driven out by force from their towns and villages.

Israel was established by the newly formed United Nations after the end of World War II by the active support of the victors of the war, including Great Britain, the United States, Russia, and other member countries. The 1947 UN Partition Plan gave the Jewish Zionist minority of Palestine the larger share of the land, leaving the Palestinian Arab majority, both Muslim and Christian, the smaller share. Although the Palestinians had nothing to do with the Holocaust in Europe, they were forced to pay a heavy price with the loss of their homeland to the new State of Israel.

The Palestinian *Nakba* shattered Palestinian life, upended the dreams of thousands, and turned people's lives upside down. Tens of thousands of Palestinians were condemned to a miserable life in refugee camps on the West Bank; the Gaza Strip; the countries of

Jordan, Lebanon, and Syria; and the rise of diaspora communities throughout the world.

The 1948 *Nakba* was the first and basic root cause of the conflict.

2. The 1967 War

According to the 1947 United Nations Partition Plan, Israel was supposed to be established on 57 percent of the land of Palestine, but in the 1948 war the Zionist militias conquered 78 percent of the land of Palestine and refused to retreat. In the 1967 War the Israeli army occupied the rest of Palestine, i.e., the West Bank including East Jerusalem and the Gaza Strip, as well as large swaths of land from Egypt, Syria, Lebanon, and Jordan.

3. The first *intifada* (Arabic for "shaking off" or "uprising") of 1987

After forty years of life under Israeli occupation, the continuous confiscation of their land, the illegal building of Israeli settlements, the loss of all Palestine, the increase of unjust and oppressive Israeli measures, and the failure of the international community to implement UN resolutions that could have ensured a just resolution to the Israel-Palestine conflict, the Palestinian community rose up to shake off the unbearable oppression of the occupation. The nonviolent *intifada* was a clear signal that the illegal occupation must come to an end and Palestine must become free. However, due to the brutality of the Israeli army and the lack of support for Palestinian aspirations by the major Western powers, it could not be done. But the *intifada* gave the Palestinians a glimmer of hope that nonviolent resistance could be an important potent weapon for the future. The *intifada* contributed to the breaking of the psychological wall of fear of the Goliath complex of the superior Israeli military machine. It also proved that the Palestinians did not have to rely on outside powers alone, that they possessed enough internal resources— ingenuity, creativity, courage, and stamina, as well as powerful ability and determination—to actively resist the occupation through nonviolent means.

The Emergence of Two Movements

The Palestinian *intifada* led to the emergence of two movements from within the Palestinian community: Hamas and Palestinian

Liberation Theology (Sabeel). Hamas is an acronym for the movement of Islamic resistance[17] that came into being during the first weeks of the *intifada*. Its founder was Sheikh Ahmad Yassin from Gaza.

After the *intifada* started, Palestinian Liberation Theology emerged as a movement in Jerusalem as a result of the publication of *Justice, and Only Justice*. The name Sabeel was adopted a few years later.[18] The objective of the two movements was the end of the illegal Israeli occupation and the liberation of our Palestinian people. I believe both movements emerged spontaneously in response to the mounting Israeli oppression.

Looking back in hindsight, Sabeel emerged as a nonviolent movement. After Sunday worship services at St. George's Episcopal Cathedral in Jerusalem, the Palestinian community of faith came together to wrestle with the question, "What should be our response to the ongoing Israeli injustice and oppression of our people?" As a result of our ongoing discussion, we began to see Jesus Christ as our liberator par excellence. Jesus said, "I am the way, the truth, and the life" (John 14:6). We began to understand that to follow in the footsteps of Jesus is to walk the way of love, truth, justice, and mercy. To follow Jesus is to choose the way of nonviolence.

This historical background necessitated the rise of Palestinian Liberation Theology.

Essential Themes for Palestinian Liberation Theology

The Concept of God

Palestinian Liberation Theology began by surveying and analyzing the political and religious reality on the ground in Israel/Palestine. It then critiqued the popular theology of many Palestinian people of the day who had given up on God, believing that our loss of Palestine and the tragedy of the *Nakba* had happened by God's will and that

---

[17] I was relatively new in Jerusalem, and I noticed that the Israeli army showed more tolerance toward the Hamas resisters. Later, many people felt it was Israel's way of undermining the Fatah party.

[18] *Sabeel* is an Arabic word that means "the way, the path," as well as "a spring of fresh and life-giving water."

the pain and suffering of our people were the results of a biased god who favored "his people Israel." It was essential to address our flawed concept and understanding of God. When discussing and wrestling with this, we made it clear that the God whom we have come to know in Jesus Christ is the God of love, righteousness, and justice who stands with the oppressed and against the oppressors. This is the authentic God of the Bible, the liberator God who champions the weak and vulnerable and leads them into liberation.

The injustice and oppression that befell us was due to the conspiring and conniving of people in power who, due to Zionist manipulation and the untenable theology of Christian Zionism, were attempting to decide the political future of Palestine. At the same time, the indigenous people of Palestine were crying for self-determination while Jewish Zionists and Western Christian Zionists were pushing for the creation of Israel. Various honorable and dishonorable factors were active in the hearts and minds of the people of power—the disregard of the rights and well-being of the people of the land, the Palestinians, versus empathy toward the future of millions of Jewish Holocaust victims, mixed with the hubris of the colonialists and imperialists. The *Nakba* was the result of evil decisions taken by the victors of World War II.

The Bible

The Bible has been the object of much misuse and abuse, and without the help of a hermeneutic it becomes difficult to correctly understand and interpret it. We know from our own Christian history how the Bible has been used to justify war, slavery, abuse, discrimination, the death penalty, and many other evils.

Christians must also differentiate between the written word in the Bible and the living and incarnate Word of God, i.e., Jesus Christ. We also believe that God's love for people is all-inclusive and unconditional regardless of race, ethnicity, sex, or gender. Once we are able to grasp and affirm the comprehensiveness of God's love, we can be better able to live our Christian life in loving God and neighbor.

I also believe that the prophetic tradition was picked up by Jesus, who repeatedly drew attention to the essence of the prophetic. "Woe to you, scribes and Pharisees, hypocrites! For you tithe mint and dill and cumin, and have neglected the weightier matters of the law, justice and mercy and faith. These you ought to have done, without neglecting the others" (Matthew 23: 23). Many Christian leaders are unwilling today to lift their prophetic voice against the injustice and oppression of the government of Israel's illegal occupation of the Palestinian territories.

Bible and Land

One of the major aspects of the conflict which Palestinian Liberation Theology addresses is the question of the land. In fact, when one looks at the Palestine/Israel conflict from a religious perspective, the theology of land constitutes the heart of the matter. Land theology stands at the center of a Palestinian Liberation Theology. The whole world, including the land, belongs to God. All of us humans are like strangers and tenants entrusted by God to use and care for it (Leviticus 25:23), for our use and others'. This theological idea is foundational and carries with it the principle of stewardship and responsibility before God, but in reality Israel has been confiscating Palestinian land as well as denying and negating Palestinian rights to their land.

From the Palestinian Liberation Theology perspective, there are various topics in the Bible that need to be carefully studied. Some of these are the tribal vs. the universal and global, the exclusive vs. the inclusive, and the nationalist vs. the prophetic. Palestinian Liberation Theology emphasizes that the general movement in the Bible is from the tribal, exclusive, and nationalist understanding of God and the land to a more universal, inclusive, and prophetic understanding. In fact, the prophetic breaks through the tribal and exclusive and the nationalist, emphasizing God's concern for justice and truth for all, including the poor and the marginalized in society.

Palestinian Liberation Theology considers the book of Jonah to contain the essence of a meaningful theology of land in the Hebrew scriptures, our Old Testament. Written toward the end of the Old

Testament period, the gifted writer uses Jonah, an Israelite prophet remembered for his bigotry and narrow nationalism, to drive home to the reader, through this allegory, God's inclusive love and care for all people and lands, regardless of race or ethnicity. The writer of Jonah critiques three exclusive popular theologies of his day, namely, the theology of God, the theology of the people of God, and the theology of the land. The writer makes clear that God is the God of the whole world and has never restricted God's activities to the people of Israel alone. Moreover, God is the God of justice who demands justice and mercy from all. God shows no partiality to any one ethnic or racial group. God's love encompasses all of humanity. Even the Assyrians who were Israel's worst enemies were not outside God's purview. God's care and compassion embraces others who repent and return to God. As to the land, God's activities and presence are not limited to one land. All lands are part of God's world, which God has created and loved and redeemed in Jesus Christ.

In many ways the New Testament theology of land follows from that of the book of Jonah. The New Testament moves beyond an exclusive theology of God, people, and land. God is the God who loves all people (John 3:16), and Jesus' ministry is not limited to Jews but is extended equally to Romans, Greeks, Samaritans, Canaanites, and others. The people of God are not limited to the offspring of Abraham, Isaac, and Jacob but extended to all those who believe (John 1: 12–13). In Jesus Christ the whole world is sanctified, and God's love and mercy encompass the whole world.

Jerusalem

In addressing the issue of Jerusalem, Palestinian Liberation Theology started by looking at two Old Testament texts. The first comes from the book of Nehemiah 2:19–20, which reflects the most exclusive vision for Jerusalem. Nehemiah tells some non-Jewish inhabitants of the land, "…you have no share or claim or historic right in Jerusalem." In its historic context, such words represent a very narrow and exclusive position regarding the city.

Psalm 87, on the other hand, represents a very inclusive position of the city. I believe Psalm 87 critiques the position of Nehemiah and offers us a model and a vision that is more worthy of Jerusalem in the twenty-first century. It presents God standing at the gate of the city and welcoming people of the various ethnic backgrounds, including some of the staunchest enemies of the ancient Israelites.

Today's Jerusalem is equally holy to the three monotheistic religions: Judaism, Christianity, and Islam. Psalm 87 can inspire a vision for the sharing of Jerusalem. It is an amazing tribute to an inspired writer who hundreds of years before the coming of Christ saw the need for an inclusive approach to the city of Jerusalem.

The Way of Nonviolence

Although there are biblical texts that reflect primitive concepts of God as partisan, narrow, violent, and exclusive, Palestinian Liberation Theology believes the essential nature of God as Jesus showed us is the God of nonviolence, peace, and love.

Palestinian Liberation Theology rejects the way of violence and critiques the way many Christians, after the fourth century, militarized and weaponized Jesus and moved the church into Christendom, waging wars under the banner of the cross and killing people in the name of Christ. Since the establishment of the State of Israel, the Israeli government has chosen to walk the way of Israeldom. This is the way of violence and war and can never lead to a permanent peace with security for all.

What, then, was the way of Jesus?

1) to stand for justice and truth without picking up the sword, to resist evil without using evil methods;
2) to rise above the ways of the world without abandoning involvement and commitment to the poor and oppressed;
3) to seek the humanity of the oppressor without losing integrity by appeasement or collaboration; and

4)   to love and worship God without adhering to a strict and closed religion.[19]

Political Vision for the Resolution of the Conflict

Palestinian Liberation Theology has courageously proclaimed a vision for a just peace for Palestine and Israel. How do we see the future of the conflict and the prospects for peace?

Palestinian Liberation Theology has made it clear that although the one-state solution is the ideal for Palestine/Israel—a one democratic state that gives all of its citizens equal rights and demands equal responsibilities of all of its Jewish, Muslim, and Christian citizens—it needs to be preceded by the two-state solution in accordance with UN resolutions and international law.

Despite the fact that the Israeli right-wing government has practically destroyed the possibility of the two-state solution, I still believe that it can be salvaged, even at the end of the recent Israeli war against Gaza. To begin with, it is significant to insist that only justice as demanded by international law and the implementation of UN resolutions can be the best guarantee for peace and security for both Palestine and Israel.

1.   The borders of the Palestinian state must be the pre-war 1967 borders; any border adjustments must be in favor of the Palestinian state.

2.   An elevated highway and rail system needs to be built between Gaza and the West Bank under the control of the United Nations for a temporary period of time. This bridge must be financed by Israel, the U.S., Britain, and their friends.

3.   Palestinian Liberation Theology boldly proposes that, in principle, there should be no objection to allowing a few of the Jewish settlers who for special religious reasons

---

[19] Naim Ateek, *A Palestinian Christian Cry for Reconciliation* (Maryknoll: Orbis, 2008), 95–96.

would like to remain living in Palestine under Palestinian rule and eventually become Palestinian citizens. All other settlers must be rehoused inside the Green Line (the 1949–1967 borders) in Israel. In their place, priority needs to be given to the Palestinian refugees who would live in their stead. This is the only way to redeem the illegal settlements.

4. The right of return of refugees must be resolved in accordance with international law, according to UN Resolution 194 (1948). Peace based on justice is a realistic possibility if the government of Israel shows willingness to respect and implement the demands of international law.

5. Jerusalem must become a city shared by both Palestine and Israel and governed equitably by a special UN commission that includes Palestinians, Israelis, and representatives of the UN and the international community.

6. All holy places must be protected and their integrity secured, especially al-Aqsa Mosque for Muslims, the Church of the Resurrection (Holy Sepulchre) for Christians, and the Western Wall for Jews.

7. After a determined number of years and an "aggressive" peace education and healing, Palestine and Israel would move together to building one state on the basis of equal democracy with a confederation/federation of states where Jerusalem would become the federal capital.

Finally, Palestinian Liberation Theology does not stop with the establishment of the State of Palestine. It must work for the achievement of reconciliation and even forgiveness.

For more Bible studies and biblical analysis relating to Palestinian Liberation Theology, please read Rev. Dr. Ateek's books on the subject. They are listed in the Further Reading section of this book.

DISCUSSION QUESTIONS

1. Palestinian Liberation Theology rejects the way of violence, much like other liberation theologies. What are some examples you've seen of successful nonviolent resistance movements?

2. Rev. Dr. Ateek states: "Palestinian Liberation Theology does not stop with the establishment of the State of Palestine. It must work for the achievement of reconciliation and even forgiveness." What do you imagine this might look like?

3. Palestinian Liberation Theology seeks not only justice, but also reconciliation. What would reconciliation look like in the context of Israel/Palestine? As those living in the United States or Canada, how can we accompany and promote a path to reconciliation?

4. The Exodus story was a key text in the Liberation Theology emerging from Latin America but is also the text cited to justify the taking of land in Palestine. How do you see Christian Zionism, explored in chapter 6, as in tension with a Palestinian theology of liberation?

CHAPTER 9

Antisemitism

Dr. Peter Makari

"Teacher, which commandment in the law is the greatest?" He said to him, "'You shall love the Lord your God with all your heart and with all your soul and with all your mind.' This is the greatest and first commandment. And a second is like it: 'You shall love your neighbor as yourself.' On these two commandments hang all the Law and the Prophets."

Matthew 22:36–40 (NRSVUE)

Antisemitism is broadly understood to mean any attitude or action that discriminates or harms someone who is Jewish because of their Jewishness. Antisemitism has a long history spanning centuries—even millennia—leading up to the twentieth century and the Holocaust (or Shoah) but has persisted since, despite the world having seen the horrific results of such attitudes and policies.

The word "Semite" comes from the name of one of Noah's sons in the Bible, Shem. The term "Semitic" was introduced in the late eighteenth century to refer to speakers of the family of Semitic languages in the western Asia and eastern African regions, which include Hebrew, Arabic, Aramaic, Akkadian, and Amharic. The link among the group of people is limited to language, and "Semitic" should not be understood as a racial or ethnic designation. Even so, antisemitism has come to be limited specifically to anti-Jewish attitudes and actions.

Anti-Jewish attitudes take many forms, including religious, economic, and social. Religious antisemitism has been manifested historically from within Christianity, including Jewish rejection of Jesus as the messiah and blaming Jews for killing Jesus. At the same time, the imperial Roman Empire mocked Jesus when he was crucified, marking his cross with the letters "INRI," a Latin acronym meaning "Jesus of Nazareth, King of the Jews." Such religious antisemitism carried forward through the centuries into the Spanish Inquisition of the fifteenth century, when Jews (and Muslims) in Iberia were persecuted, expelled, and killed. Supersessionism—the idea that God's covenant with the Israelites was superseded (or replaced) and therefore negated by Christianity—is another example of antisemitism. And the theology of Christian Zionism, or pre-millennial dispensationalism, is antisemitic as it requires the conversion of Jews to Christianity at the time of Christ's coming, or else they would suffer in eternal damnation.

Economic antisemitism refers to the idea that Jewish people control the banks and contributes to the persistence of stereotypes of Jewish people as miserly or greedy. Social antisemitism views Jews as less polite, less cultured, and socially inferior. All of these result in attitudes and actions that verge on racism.

Such attitudes led to the promulgation and implementation of laws and policies in Europe that ghettoized Jewish members of society, restricting where they could live, how much property they could own, what jobs they could hold, and how and when they could worship. Even though many of these laws were repealed in the early 1800s, the attitudes persisted. Jews were further persecuted by the National Socialist German Worker's Party (the Nazi Party), which forced them to labor and death camps to eliminate Jews and other peoples who were seen as inferior to the Aryan race. The Holocaust resulted in the deaths of more than six million Jews in Europe. Antisemitic attitudes limited the numbers of European Jews who could immigrate to the UK, the U.S., and other places, even in the midst of such horror.

Antisemitic attitudes have persisted into the twenty-first century, including as part of the idea of the "Great Replacement Theory," a white nationalist ideology attributed to French author Renaud Camus. The theory suggests that white Christian European populations would be replaced by others, including non-Christian, non-white people, primarily through immigration and demographic changes. The ideas of replacement theory include antisemitic and Islamophobic attitudes. Such attitudes were on display in Charlottesville, Virginia, in August 2017 during a demonstration against the removal of a statue of Confederate general Robert E. Lee at a rally called "Unite the Right." During the demonstration, which became violent, protestors were heard chanting, "Jews will not replace us!"

The declaration of the establishment of the State of Israel in Palestine in 1948 purported indeed, in part, to offer a place of refuge for European Jews fleeing persecution. There, European Jews joined small communities of Palestinian Jews who lived alongside the majority Palestinian Muslim and Christian community. Even so, Palestinians (and others) believe atonement for European antisemitism should not have come at the expense of Palestinians.

The practices and policies of the State of Israel vis-à-vis the Palestinian people have also drawn criticism from many corners of the globe and from many communities. Established in 1948 and adopting the Nation State Law in 2018, Israel defines itself as a Jewish state, despite more than one-fifth of its citizenry being non-Jewish. Since the 1967 War, Israel has occupied and controlled a Palestinian population in East Jerusalem, the West Bank, and Gaza that does not have Israeli citizenship nor the associated rights but lives under an Israeli military regime. Criticism of Israel's policies and practices is often characterized by Israeli officials and its defenders as antisemitic because it is directed at the Jewish state and because, they would say, Israel is being held to a different standard than other countries in the world.

Most recently, the United Church of Christ adopted a resolution in 2021 called "Declaration for a Just Peace Between Palestine and Israel." In it, the General Synod "reject[ed] the idea that any criticism of policies of the State of Israel is inherently antisemitic, in confession that some criticism is antisemitic in intent or impact." In 2023, at its General Assembly, the Christian Church (Disciples of Christ) passed a resolution called "Compelled to Witness," in which it "condemn[ed] speech and acts of antisemitism, and reject[ed] the notion that criticism of policies of the State of Israel is inherently antisemitic." Critique of a government's policy is not the same as hatred or bigoted attitudes toward a whole group of people. The resolutions recognize that some may criticize Israel from an anti-Jewish bias, but many Jewish Israelis and Jewish Americans, for example, are critical of Israeli policies as well.

Efforts during U.S. President Donald Trump and Joe Biden's terms to adopt the International Holocaust Remembrance Alliance definition of antisemitism have been criticized by people around the world, including Jewish leaders and intellectuals in the U.S. and Israel, because many of the supporting examples in the document cite criticism of Israel as antisemitic. They reject the idea that criticism of Israel is necessarily antisemitic while acknowledging the scourge of antisemitism that continues to exist. Alternative definitions have been proposed, including the Jerusalem Declaration on Antisemitism (2021), which does not consider support for Palestinian rights or anti-Zionism as necessarily antisemitic.

Instances of antisemitism have increased dramatically since early October 2023, following Hamas' attacks on Israel and the war Israel waged on Gaza. Jewish people as well as establishments, including businesses and synagogues, have been subject to verbal and physical harassment due to their identity. These cannot be denied, but they should not be conflated with criticism of Israeli policies and practices that have suppressed Palestinian rights for decades and have resulted the decimation of the Palestinian population and communities in Gaza in 2023–2024.

The United Church of Christ and Christian Church (Disciples of Christ) have been engaged in Jewish-Christian dialogue for decades, and issues related to antisemitism and Israel/Palestine have been part of those ecumenical dialogues. Both churches have been clear in their condemnation of antisemitism and have spoken out when instances of antisemitism have occurred, such as the mass shooting at the Tree of Life Synagogue in Pittsburgh, Pennsylvania, in October 2018. Many Disciples and UCC clergy and congregations maintain healthy relationships with rabbis and synagogues around the country.

DISCUSSION QUESTIONS

1. Where have you seen antisemitism in your church, community, and/or country? Was there a response? If so, what was it?

2. How might antisemitism appear as part of critiques of policies of the State of Israel?

3. Do you think it is possible to be critical of Israel's policies and actions without being (or being perceived as) antisemitic? Why or why not?

Section 4

Modern Day Israel/Palestine

I must admit—it is so difficult today to hold to our faith, and to hope. We cannot see Sunday. It seems an impossibility. We are swallowed by the darkness of the tomb. Our strength has failed. We are weary. It is so hard to speak of the resurrection now. We are mourning. Our siblings in Gaza are literally dying from starvation. But we CANNOT lose our faith in God.

"Easter Amidst a Genocide," Rev. Dr. Munther Isaac

CHAPTER 10

Colonialism and Settler Colonialism

Rebekah Choate

Whoever is faithful in a very little is faithful also in much, and whoever is dishonest in a very little is dishonest also in much. If, then, you have not been faithful with the dishonest wealth, who will entrust to you the true riches? And if you have not been faithful with what belongs to another, who will give you what is your own? No slave can serve two masters, for a slave will either hate the one and love the other or be devoted to the one and despise the other. You cannot serve God and wealth.

Luke 16:10–13 (NRSVUE)

Classical colonialism is the domination of a people or area by a foreign state or nation—the practice of extending and maintaining a nation's political and economic control over another people or area. An example of a classical colonial system is that of the Belgian kingdom in what is now the Democratic Republic of Congo. The Belgians were interested solely in the material wealth generated by the raw materials in Congo, first rubber then diamonds, gold, and other minerals. They were not interested in bringing Belgians to Congo to settle there permanently in large numbers, but their interest in material wealth led to exploitation and oppression of the Congolese people.

By contrast, settler colonialism is the invasion and occupation of a territory to permanently displace the indigenous population and replace the existing society with the society of the colonizers. A historical example of a settler colonial system is the United States and its westward expansion and subsequent genocide of the Native American population and replacement by Europeans.

Late nineteenth- and early twentieth-century political and religious leaders, including British clergy and elites like Rev. Alexander Keith and Anthony Ashley-Cooper, Lord of Shaftesbury, as well as Christian Zionists like the American William Blackstone, and Chaim Weizmann, who became Israel's first president, described the area of historic Palestine as "a land without a people for a people without a land" to promote the vision of a Jewish homeland in Palestine. They ignored the presence of the native Palestinian population who had been living there for millennia. This phrase was popular to encourage Jewish emigration and settlement.

Population transfers and settlement projects (key pieces of settler colonialism) have been illegal under international law since the Fourth Geneva Convention, signed in 1949, after the Nuremburg Trials in 1945–1946 declared them a war crime and crime against humanity. The Israeli settlements in the West Bank, Golan Heights, and those formerly in Gaza have been called illegal many times by various U.S. administrations among others, including most recently the International Court of Justice in its July 19, 2024, advisory opinion.[20] However, Israel continues to approve, establish, and construct illegal settlements, sourced in part with money and support from U.S. citizens and organizations, and even from U.S. public pension funds and other city, state, or national government-owned funds. These settlements continue to create facts on the ground that have made a two-state solution practically impossible to implement. Today Israeli settlers are about eight hundred thousand in number.

Israeli settlers work in coordination with the Israeli military to protect and expand settlements. The Israeli military first designates the land as a protected military zone, forcing those already living there to move, often by demolishing homes and property. Then temporary shelters like trailer homes or prefabricated housing are brought in with military outposts. They expand into fully-planned

---

[20] "Legal Consequences Arising from the Policies and Practices of Israel in the Occupied Palestinian Territory, Including East Jerusalem," International Court of Justice, July 19, 2024, https://www.icj-cij.org/sites/default/files/case-related/186/186-20240719-adv-01-00-en.pdf.

housing development sites, resembling a suburb with all the luxuries of a community—parks, pools, shopping areas, etc.

Once the housing units have been completed, the Israeli government heavily subsidizes the cost to buy or rent a house, thus encouraging new migrants and other Jewish Israelis to move to the settlement. Non-Jews are not permitted to live in the settlements, and if a business located in a settlement wants to hire non-Israelis to work there, workers require a special permit that allows them to travel to and enter the settlement.

Israeli settlers are governed by Israeli civil law, while neighboring Palestinians living in the same West Bank area are governed by Israeli military law. This unequal system means that most Israeli settlers are given light sentences, if they are charged with a crime, in civil court. Meanwhile, Palestinians can be detained without trial for an indefinite period without charges in military courts. Israeli settlers thus are emboldened to attack Palestinians and destroy their crops and land, particularly by uprooting olive trees. In many documented instances, the Israeli military has provided protection and support to the settlers who uproot trees and attack Palestinians.

There are two types of Israeli settlers—those who are ideological and those who become settlers for economic reasons. The ideological settlers firmly believe in the occupation based on their understanding of Hebrew scriptures. These settlers are more extreme and often commit acts of physical violence against Palestinians to take their land. Many of these settlers erect outposts deep in the West Bank, which even the Israeli government has called illegal, but without consequence, and eventually they become "normal" and "legalized."

Economic settlers are those drawn to the low-cost housing and interest-free loans and are mostly located in long-established settlements nearer the Green Line (the 1949 armistice line, also known as the 1967 border) but still located on occupied Palestinian territories. Many of these economic settlers are recent Jewish immigrants to Israel and have no particularly strong ideological views regarding the Jewish state. Both types of settlers participate in the Israeli settler colonial project, however, regardless of motivation. Increasingly, these distinctions are disappearing as settlers, backed by the Israeli state, have become bolder and more aggressive in their harassment of Palestinians and their property. All settlements and settlers are in violation of international law.

DISCUSSION QUESTIONS

1. What do you understand to be the key differences between classical colonialism, as seen in the Democratic Republic of Congo, as opposed to settler colonialism, as seen in South Africa or Israel/Palestine? Why do you think settlements and settler colonialism are now illegal under international law?

2. How would you feel if your land and home were taken and given over to someone else?

3. Global Ministries core values include community. How does settler colonialism go against this value?

4. Global Ministries embraces a post-colonial approach to mission and post-colonial theology. How do you understand post-colonial theology to speak to current iterations of settler colonialism?

CHAPTER 11

Apartheid

Krista Johnson Weicksel

That there may be no dissension within the body, but the members may have the same care for one another. If one member suffers, all suffer together with it; if one member is honored, all rejoice together with it.

1 Corinthians 12: 25–26

We know all too well that our freedom is incomplete without the freedom of the Palestinians.

Nelson Mandela

For more than two decades, some UCC and Disciples partners in the Middle East region have been using the apartheid framework to describe Israeli policies and practices. Using the apartheid framework in this context is not intended to be a provocation nor to simply compare the South African experience of apartheid to the Palestinian experience of living under occupation. Instead, using the apartheid framework is meant to apply the international legal definition of the crime of apartheid to the realities on the ground today in Israel and Palestine.

Sabeel Ecumenical Liberation Theology Center founder Rev. Dr. Naim Ateek wrote in 2008, "For some time now, I have been advocating the use of a Hebrew word *'hafrada'* as a way of describing the Israeli form of apartheid." The word *hafrada*, which translates as "separation" in Hebrew, is already used in Israel to describe the policies the government of Israel and many people wish to have. In fact, in the Israeli media the wall is referred to as the *hafrada* barrier, as the separation barrier, not the security barrier as it is often referred to in the West, self-identifying a policy of separation. In Afrikaans the word apartheid literally means "separation," though in South Africa it eventually acquired a more sinister connotation. Ateek explains, "Although *hafrada*—separation—in Palestine is proposed under the guise of security, many of us know that it expresses racism ... is conjuring up racist attitudes and not simply a desire for separation."

In addition to Sabeel, which first began speaking of conditions for Palestinians as apartheid in its Jerusalem Document (2000), other Disciples and UCC partners have also named the policies and practices as apartheid for several years.

Article III of the International Convention on the Suppression and Punishment of the Crime of Apartheid defines the crime of apartheid as applying to "inhuman acts committed for the purpose of establishing and maintaining domination by one racial group over another racial group and systematically oppressing them." Likewise, Article 7 of the 2002 Rome Statute of the International Criminal Court lists apartheid as one of several crimes against humanity. The crime of apartheid is defined as inhumane acts such as torture, imprisonment, or the persecution of an identifiable group on political, racial, national, ethnic, cultural, religious, or other grounds "committed in the context of an institutionalized regime of systematic oppression and domination by one racial group over any other racial group or groups and committed with the intention of maintaining that regime."

In 2021 B'Tselem, a prominent Israeli human rights group and UCC and Disciples partner, released a groundbreaking report called "A Regime of Jewish Supremacy from the Jordan River to the Mediterranean Sea: This Is Apartheid." It identified and named several areas where Israeli policy and practice meet the legal definition of the crime of apartheid. These include Jewish-only immigration, appropriating land for Jewish populations at the expense of Palestinian presence; restricting Palestinian freedom of movement; and denial of Palestinian political participation. Their 2022 report "Not a Vibrant Democracy. This Is Apartheid" states, "B'Tselem rejects the perception of Israel as a democracy (inside the Green Line) that simultaneously upholds a temporary military occupation (beyond it)." B'Tselem reached the conclusion that the bar for naming the Israeli regime as an apartheid regime has been met after considering the accumulation of policies and laws that Israel devised to entrench its control over Palestinians.

Alongside B'Tselem, respected international human rights organizations Human Rights Watch (2021) and Amnesty international (2022) both released reports outlining how Israeli policies had met the criteria to be classified as the crime of apartheid. The Human Rights Watch report concluded that the Israeli government has demonstrated an intent to maintain the domination of Jewish Israelis over Palestinians across Israel and the occupied Palestinian territories (oPt). The report states: "Intent has been coupled with systematic oppression of Palestinians and inhumane acts committed against them. When these three elements occur together, they amount to the crime of apartheid."[21]

The United Church of Christ in 2021 and the Christian Church (Disciples of Christ) in 2023 became two of the first three mainline Protestant churches to pass resolutions describing the current situation in Israel/Palestine explicitly as apartheid. The Presbyterian Church (USA) also adopted the framework in 2022. These respective resolutions came in response to reports and calls from partners in the region. Specifically, Kairos Palestine published a watershed letter called "Cry for Hope: A Call to Decisive Action" on July 1, 2020. The "Cry for Hope" letter called upon "all Christians and on churches at congregational, denominational, national, and global ecumenical levels to engage in a process of study, reflection and confession concerning

---

[21] Human Rights Watch. "A Threshold Crossed." April 27, 2021. https://www.hrw.org/report/2021/04/27/threshold-crossed/israeli-authorities-and-crimes-apartheid-and-persecution

the historic and systemic deprivation of the rights of the Palestinian people, and the use of the Bible by many to justify and support this oppression." It went on to declare, "As followers of Jesus, our response to ideologies of exclusivity and apartheid is to uphold a vision of inclusivity and equality for all peoples of the land and to persistently struggle to bring this about."

Two years later, also published by Kairos Palestine and its Global Kairos for Justice network, "A Dossier on Israeli Apartheid: A Pressing Call to Churches Around the World" said, "Now is the time for the global Church—and each of its constituent bodies—to recognize Israel as an apartheid state and to actively and nonviolently resist its apartheid laws, policies and practices."

The report went on to say, "To call Israel an apartheid regime is not a political epithet, nor does it require comparisons with South Africa, but an examination of the facts on the ground, which fulfills the legal elements established for the crime of Apartheid. These elements are so clearly there." The resource clearly and thoroughly examines each of the elements of the crime of apartheid and offers churches a way to learn more and dig deeper. It concludes with a call to action:

"What will you do about it?" We Palestinians ask the Church, "How will you respond? Are you able to help us get our freedom back?" Your answer shapes our future. For Palestinians, our struggle for freedom is a matter of utmost importance. We are talking about people's lives and livelihood. We are talking about our very existence on the land of our ancestors.

How can we, as Christians, work to answer this call?

Consider joining the Apartheid-Free Campaign, which invites congregations, faith groups, and organizations to sign an apartheid-free pledge to stand in solidarity with the Palestinian people and build an anti-apartheid movement in North America. The UCC was a founding member of this campaign, and both the UCC and Disciples have endorsed the campaign.

> ### Apartheid-Free Pledge
>
> WE AFFIRM our commitment to freedom, justice, and equality for the Palestinian people and all people;
>
> WE OPPOSE all forms of racism, bigotry, discrimination, and oppression; and
>
> WE DECLARE ourselves an apartheid-free community and to that end,
>
> WE PLEDGE to join others in working to end all support to Israel's apartheid regime, settler colonialism, and military occupation.

DISCUSSION QUESTIONS

1. What do you think of when you hear the word apartheid? What types of policies or situations do you see?

2. Based on the legal definition of the crime of apartheid, do you see it possibly occurring anywhere else in the world or in history?

3. Is understanding Israeli treatment of Palestinians as apartheid helpful framing for you? Why or why not?

4. Why would apartheid be considered a sin? How does it limit and harm the flourishing of God's people and creation?

CHAPTER 12

U.S. Military Aid to Israel

Rebekah Choate

Blessed are the peacemakers, for they will be called children of God.

Matthew 5:9 (NRSVUE)

Every year the United States sends about $3.8 billion in military aid to Israel, which deploys one of the most advanced militaries in the world. All other countries are required to use U.S. military aid to purchase weapons, equipment, and services from U.S. defense and weapons companies. Israel has an exemption from this requirement.

Israel has received more U.S. military aid than any other country since World War II. In recent years U.S. military funding to Israel has been outlined in ten-year memorandums of understanding. President Barack Obama signed the most recent MOU in 2016 for the fiscal years 2019–2028, pledging $33 billion in foreign military funding and $5 billion for missile defense funding over the ten years.

Any transfers of military equipment to a foreign government are subject to U.S. law. Under the Arms Control Exports Act, the president must notify Congress about weapons sales that are over certain dollar amounts (for Israel those limits are any major defense equipment of $25 million or more, any defense articles or services of $100 million or more, or design and construction services of $300 million or more) and give Congress time to review the sale (fifteen days for Israel). Congress can block the sale of weapons, but it has never done so for any country. In certain cases the president can bypass Congress if it is considered a national security emergency. President Biden has used this authority to send weapons to both Ukraine since Russia's invasion in 2022 and Israel since October 7, 2023. However, there have been more than one hundred transactions below the congressional reporting limits to Israel since October 7, 2023, according to reporting in *The Washington Post*.[22] Among the weapons sold were precision-guided munitions, small-diameter bombs, bunker-buster rockets, and others.

Any military aid the U.S. sends to other countries is also subject to the Leahy Law. This law states that military aid cannot be sent to foreign governments or groups that commit human rights violations. Many critics, including the UCC and Disciples, believe the U.S. doesn't apply the Leahy Law consistently, particularly when it comes to Israel, but also to other countries like the Philippines.

There have been instances in the past when the U.S. has banned certain weapons sales to Israel. President Ronald Reagan banned the sale of cluster munitions to Israel for several years during the 1980s after it was determined Israel had used them on the civilian population in Lebanon during their invasion in 1982. In December 2023 President Biden banned a shipment of assault rifles to Israel as he thought there was a good chance that they would end up in the hands of extremist Israeli settler groups in the West Bank.

In 2008 Congress passed a law stating that any weapons the U.S. provides to other countries in the Middle East must not compromise Israel's qualitative military edge in relation to other countries in the region. In a few cases this has required the U.S. to provide Israel with weapons as part of larger regional arms sales. This law has also ensured that Israel is the first in the region to receive the most sophisticated U.S. weapons and systems.

Over the years there have been many concerns raised over the amount of military aid the U.S. sends to Israel. Israel routinely uses U.S.-made weapons to attack Palestinians and commit other human

---

[22] Adam Taylor, "What to know about U.S. military aid to Israel" April 2, 2024, https://www.washingtonpost.com/world/2024/04/02/us-military-aid-israel-gaza-biden/

rights abuses.[23] Israel is one of the most developed economies in the world, has one of the most advanced militaries, and has its own very profitable arms development and manufacturing industry. So the question is raised as to why it needs so much support from the U.S.

Israel has become one of the world's leading arms exporters, selling approximately $12.56 billion in defense exports in 2022. Drones accounted for 25 percent of the 2022 exports and missiles, rockets, or air defense systems for 19 percent. When marketing these weapons, Israel calls them "battle tested" because the Israeli military has been using them against Palestinians.[24]

Most countries receive allocations of U.S. military aid in quarterly installments, and the money is kept in U.S.-controlled bank accounts until the country wishes to draw down from its allocation to purchase weapons. This arrangement allows the United States greater oversight over weapons purchases and better control over the purse strings to ensure countries' compliance with U.S. laws.

Israel, however, enjoys preferential status. Since 1991 Congress has authorized Israel to receive its allocation in one lump sum and early (within thirty days of the budget's enactment). Moreover, Israel is allowed to hold these funds in a U.S. interest-bearing bank account so that Israel ends up with more than its annual allocation of $3.8 billion.

An October 5, 2012, Ecumenical Letter on Military Aid[25] signed by Disciples of Christ and UCC leaders among many others said:

As Christian leaders in the United States, it is our moral responsibility to question the continuation of unconditional U.S. financial assistance to the government of Israel. Realizing

[23] Ellen Knickmeyer, Aamer Madhani, and Matthew Lee, "US says Israel's use of US arms likely violated international law, but evidence is incomplete", AP News, May 11, 2024, https://apnews.com/article/us-israel-gaza-war-nsm-international-law-c83b6f39ce2799e5d2c473a337e2f857

[24] Sophia Goodfriend "Gaza war offers the ultimate marketing tool for Israeli arms companies" +972 Magazine, January 17, 2024, https://www.972mag.com/gaza-war-arms-companies/

[25] See the full letter: https://www.globalministries.org/wp-content/uploads/nb/legacy_url/7495/Military-aid-to-Israel-Oct-1-Final.pdf?1419969549.

a just and lasting peace will require this accountability, as continued U.S. military assistance to Israel—offered without conditions or accountability—will only serve to sustain the status quo and Israel's military occupation of the Palestinian territories.

U.S. military aid to Israel since October 7, 2023, has been robust and consistent, including $2 billion in ammunition, interceptors, and other defense technology. It has also included tank shells and artillery, various sized bombs and missiles, and a commitment to more fighter jets, as well as financial assistance in the billions of dollars.

The UCC and Disciples have spoken repeatedly against the militarization of the region and U.S. military aid to Israel in resolutions and public statements. This call has gained wider currency—even in Congress—during Israel's military campaign in Gaza since October 2023.

DISCUSSION QUESTIONS

1. Why do you think Israel has special status when it comes to receiving U.S. foreign military aid? Do you think there are other countries that have special status as well?

2. U.S. military aid to other countries is a product of the U.S. military industrial complex that arose out of World War II. Why do you think that system has been maintained, and can you envision a world without this system?

Section 5

Moving Forward

The resurrection urges us to rise and act! Because we know that the final word belongs to God, we rise and act. We build. We preach love because we know love wins. We preach peace because peace wins. We preach life because death is defeated. Jesus stared death in the face and defeated it. And therefore, we rise and act.

"Easter Amidst a Genocide," Rev. Dr. Munther Isaac

CHAPTER 13

Palestine: Toward a Paradigm Shift

Rev. Dr. Mitri Raheb

This chapter is based on excerpts from Rev. Dr. Mitri Raheb's book Decolonizing Palestine: The Land, the People, the Bible *(New York: Orbis Press, 2023). Printed with permission.*

Throughout the past hundred years, Israel has used different means to further its settler colonial project: sometimes through conquest and land colonization, other times through illegal laws or economic pressures. Throughout these years biblical mythistory has provided a discourse depicting the native Palestinian Arabs as aliens or savage terrorists and Jewish Israelis as civilized, democratic, or a start-up nation. To defend the settler colonial project, Israel created a police state that was granted extraordinary power over the native people. The ultimate goal for Israel has been to control the whole geography of historic Palestine while confining the Palestinian population into different forms of Bantustans as an interim stage toward ultimate ethnic cleansing. Behind all of these endeavors lies a settler colonial mindset and policy.

While some churches in Canada, Australia, and certain parts of the United States are confronting their settler colonial heritage, Israel is advancing its settler colonial project at a rapid pace. These churches now acknowledge that they stand on land owned by first nations whereas Israeli settlers and colonizers are grabbing land from defenseless Palestinian families throughout the West Bank. The Judaization of Jerusalem is a story of settler colonialism that aims to erase the Arab and Palestinian presence from the city. The story of al-Aqsa is a story of settler colonialism in which the goal is to replace an Arab Muslim shrine and worshippers with a "third Jewish temple."

All these activities are based on a biblical discourse that gives the settlers the requisite theological rationale. A *hasbara* (Hebrew, "public diplomacy" or "propaganda") apparatus works to perpetuate the image of Palestinians as terrorists whose rockets deliberately kill civilians, while Israeli airstrikes are conducted with "surgical precision," even if fifty-plus Palestinian children are bombed "by mistake."[26] This Israeli settler colonial endeavor has to be seen as the last chapter of the Western settler colonial project, taking place today in the twenty-first century in Palestine. It continues to be serviced and powered by the motherland: the Anglo-Saxon world.

The Empire at Work

The colonization of Palestine in modern history was facilitated by the British Empire through the Balfour Declaration and continues to be made possible by the American empire. In this sense, the imperial project that started in the mid-nineteenth century continues today. Thus, we need to see the State of Israel as an integral part of empire or empire by proxy. Today, empire is bigger than one state, nation, or military power. The Accra Confession[27] defined empire as the convergence of economic, political, cultural, geographic, and military imperial interests, systems and networks that seek to dominate political power and economic wealth. It typically forces and facilitates the flow of wealth and power from vulnerable persons, communities, and countries to the more powerful. Empire today is linked to Western hegemony and white supremacy that built its wealth over centuries of colonialism and also to a vast military industry. Empire today is linked to the so-called Judeo-Christian tradition that became a code for cultural and ethnic supremacy. Israel is part of this empire and is sustained by it with supplies of "hardware" such as submarines, F-35 fighter jets, and the Iron Dome missile defense system, as well as political and diplomatic backing. Israel is seen as part of the Western

---

[26] PBS News Hour "Netanyahu acknowledges 'tragic mistake' after Rafah strike kills at least 45 Palestinians" May 27, 2024, https://www.pbs.org/newshour/world/netanyahu-acknowledges-tragic-mistake-after-rafah-strike-kills-at-least-45-palestinians

[27] https://wcrc.eu/about/accra-confession/

world, serving the latter's interests as one of its main allies. Today Israel is the seventh-biggest exporter of military and security equipment worldwide. Additionally, the empire provides Israel with the "software" of a biblical blueprint that paints colonial practices with theological justifications of a "promised land" and "chosen people." Another aspect of the software is the depiction of Israel as a shining example of the so-called democratic world and Western values.

The Ecumenical Deal

The Jewish liberation theologian Marc Ellis coined the phrase "the ecumenical deal" to describe the relationship between the Jewish synagogue and Christian church in the West. This ecumenical deal usually referred to post-Holocaust interfaith ecumenical dialogue where Jews and Christians have mended their relationship. Israel has been central in this dialogue. Christians supported Israel as repentance for antisemitism and the Holocaust. As Israel became more controversial due to its abuse of Palestinians, Christians remained silent. Failure to support or, worse, criticism of Israeli policies, was viewed by the Jewish dialogue participants as an expression of antisemitism. The dialogue became a deal: silence on the part of Christians earns no criticism of antisemitism from Jews. The interfaith ecumenical deal was also part of a larger political deal in the American political scene. Any criticism of Israel by a political figure was their death knell, and accusations of antisemitism were the bullets.[28]

In 2012 Marc Ellis declared this ecumenical deal dead. While several mainline Protestant churches like the United Church of Christ, the Presbyterian Church (USA), and the Christian Church (Disciples of Christ) are today more articulate than ever, most of the mega and influential congregations in the main American cities are sticking to the ecumenical deal, a deal that is still alive and even thriving in many European countries like Germany, Holland, and even the human rights champion country Sweden.

---

[28] Marc H. Ellis, "Exile and the Prophetic: The Interfaith Ecumenical Deal Is Dead," *Mondoweiss*, November 12, 2012, https://mondoweiss.net/2012/11/exile-and-the-prophetic-the-interfaith-ecumenical-deal-is-dead/.

What is true for the churches is true for mainline Protestant theology. As Julia M. O'Brian puts it:

For typical US mainline Protestants, an interpretation of a biblical text is convincing and compelling if they hear it as:

- Liberal, supporting universal human rights, especially for those whom they recognize as historically oppressed, and even more especially women.

- Scientific, objectively verified by text itself, even more by historians and archeologists.

- Savvy, sufficiently skeptical of human bias.

- Supportive of Judaism and supported by Jewish readers.

An interpretation is problematic if they hear it as:

- Socially conservative, unconcerned with the improvement of this world, especially the status of women.

- Fundamentalist or overly pious, accepting biblical testimony at face value.

- Ideological, promoting only one side of a conflict that they believe is multi-faceted.

- Challenging what Jews say about the Old Testament.[29]

This hermeneutic, or interpretive, lens has led to a Judaization of Christian theological writings and literature. While it was important to combat the earlier anti-Jewish traditions in Christian theology, the pro-Jewish hermeneutics created, consciously or unconsciously, a pro-Israel attitude with an anti-Palestinian twist embedded in it. This philo-Semitic Christian theology ran parallel to the Judaization of the land of Palestine and in some cases provided a theological cushion for Israeli practices. The settler colonial narrative that celebrates the colonizers while criminalizing the natives as savages was particularly

---

[29] Julia O'Brien, "The Hermeneutical Predicament: Why We Do Not Read the Bible in the Same Way and Why It Matters to Palestinian Advocacy," in *The Biblical Text in the Context of Occupation: Towards a New Hermeneutics of Liberation,* ed. Mitri Raheb (Bethlehem: Diyar, 2012), 169–70.

apparent in the film industry. Jack Shaheen, a scholar who dedicated his career to analyzing stereotypes in Hollywood films, examined over 1,100 films for his groundbreaking book *Reel Bad Arab: How Hollywood Vilifies a People*[30] and found that Americans were entertained by these negative depictions of Arabs, Palestinians, and Muslims, which amounts to propaganda.

History and Power

Churches feel that they must side with Israel because of what happened to the Jews in Europe during the Holocaust. Their declared rationale is that they have learned a lesson from history. This assumption needs to be questioned. Yes, maybe the church has become sensitive to anti-Jewish traditions within it, but the church still feels more comfortable in siding with those in power. The Israel lobby is very strong and actively rewards those who follow them, while punishing those who follow their conscience. It remains very costly to side with the weak and oppressed, and the price can be one's career, reputation, and even life. Dietrich Bonhoeffer was part of a tiny Confessing Church that dared to challenge the powers of his time, and he paid with his life. While Bonhoeffer is widely celebrated, almost as a Protestant saint, very few dare to walk in his footsteps today and challenge the Israeli state and its lobbies embedded in church and society.

What lessons are learned from history if churches and political groups are fearful of the Israel lobby and side with the powerful State of Israel against the oppressed Palestinian people? Another explanation for this blind support is that Western groups see Ashkenazi Israelis as members of their kin and of their own white tribe.

Apartheid

Many years ago credible politicians like President Jimmy Carter warned that without a real peace agreement the Israeli occupation would lead to an apartheid system.[31] President Carter was followed by

---

[30] Jack G. Shaheen, *Reel Bad Arabs: How Hollywood Vilifies a People*, 3rd edition (Northampton, Massachusetts: Olive Branch Press, 2012).

[31] Jimmy Carter, *Palestine: Peace Not Apartheid*, reprint edition (New York: Simon & Schuster, 2007).

Israeli politicians[32] who rang similar alarms. In the last two years several highly credible human rights organizations, including Jewish human rights organizations like B'Tselem, have declared that the threshold has already been crossed and apartheid now exists on both sides of the Green Line.[33] Human rights organizations like Human Rights Watch[34] and Amnesty International[35] have identified the situation in historic Palestine as apartheid, according to the international legal as set by the Geneva Conventions, the International Convention on the Suppression and Punishment of the Crime of Apartheid, and the Rome Statute of the International Criminal Court. Three decisive elements define the crime of apartheid: the implementation of a system of segregation based on race, religion or ethnicity designed with the intent to maintain domination by one group over another; the use of diverse legislative measures to enforce and legalize segregation; and inhumane practices and violations to impose and enforce such segregation. These three components are found in the definition of settler colonialism. Apartheid and settler colonialism are two sides of the same coin.

Toward a Paradigm Shift

Many of the same Western politicians and church leaders who shy away from supporting Palestine, both criticizing and criminalizing Palestinian resistance, are mobilizing political, financial, public relations, and military power in support of Ukraine against Russia. While they perceive the Russian invasion as a clear-cut act of atrocity that requires support for the Ukrainian people, they describe the Israeli occupation of Palestinian land as complicated, although it is clear in

---

[32] Allison Kaplan Sommer, "Ehud Barak Warns: Israel Faces 'Slippery Slope' Toward Apartheid," *Haaretz*, June 21, 2017, https://www.haaretz.com/israel-news/2017-06-21/ty-article/ehud-barak-warns-israel-on-slippery-slope-to-apartheid/0000017f-ef8b-d0f7-a9ff-efcf52ce0000.

[33] "Apartheid," B'Tselem, https://www.btselem.org/topic/apartheid.

[34] Omar Shakir, "Israeli Apartheid: 'A Threshold Crossed,'" Human Rights Watch, July 19, 2021, https://www.hrw.org/news/2021/07/19/israeli-apartheid-threshold-crossed.

[35] "Israel's Apartheid Against Palestinians," Amnesty International, February 1, 2022, https://www.amnesty.org/en/latest/campaigns/2022/02/israels-system-of-apartheid/.

international law. The description as "complicated" is used to blur the Palestinian issue and portray it as an exception to the rule. The genocide in Gaza presents a real challenge to the credibility of the entire Western world, which has not yet come to terms with the ramifications of its colonial heritage. Unfortunately, there is no indication that this will change in the short term. The West will continue to provide their ally with military hardware and theological software. The State of Israel is the seventh-largest military power worldwide, and the Jewish lobby is investing billions of dollars to silence voices that oppose the settler colonial project. It does not feel any urgency or reason to compromise. On the contrary, the Israeli establishment now sees in Gaza an opportunity to seal its deal, ethnically cleanse Palestinians in Gaza and the West Bank, and bring its settler colonial project to its ultimate completion.

Yet some cracks in the wall are visible, and the Israeli settler colonial project is failing. Palestinians will not disappear from the land where their roots lie and continue to demonstrate their unity across artificial borders alongside their determination to resist the settler colonial project with all available means. There is a young and dynamic generation of Palestinians who are articulate, passionate, skilled, and active in defending their cause. If the name of the game for Israelis is settler colonialism, the name of the game for Palestinians is resilience: *sumud.* Over the past seventy-plus years, Palestinians have shown over and over again a tremendous strength to resist, incredible forms of resilience, and creative ways to survive. The Palestinians are not moving, and they will persist in the face of the Israeli settler colonial project.

The Israeli settler colonial project constitutes not only a threat to Palestinians but also to the many Jews who desire to live in peace with the Palestinians. While the peace camp in Israel has shrunk tremendously, Jewish groups in the diaspora like Jewish Voice for Peace have recognized the harm the Israeli settler colonial project is doing to their Jewish identity and liberal outlook. They do not want to associate with the policies and settler colonial practices of the "Jewish State." They declare freely and unapologetically their solidarity and support for an end to the settler colonial project. Mass demonstrations against the war in Gaza are seen in all major capitals. Solidarity networks have been created with social justice movements like Black Lives Matter, with artists from the first nations, native Americans, and Aboriginals. Conferences focusing on Palestine are taking place in many locations. Social media is full of posts in support of Palestine. Will this bring about the desired change soon? I doubt it! Yet all these steps will continue to widen the cracks in the wall until the day that it will fall. There is no future for this settler colonial project. Palestine must be understood as one of the last anti-colonial struggles in an era regarded as post-colonial. Churches and people of faith are called today to walk the talk and to engage in the struggle to decolonize Palestine.

DISCUSSION QUESTIONS

1. Where else in the world do you see colonialism and empire still active? In what ways?

2. Rev. Dr. Raheb states that "churches feel that they must side with Israel because of what happened to the Jews in Europe during the Holocaust." Do you think that is true in your church? Is it true in the wider Christian community in your community?

3. Rev. Dr. Raheb talks about the struggle between the Israeli settler colonial project and Palestinian *sumud*, the Arabic word for resilience. Where else do you see resilience today?

4. How are you inspired to talk the talk and walk the walk to change the narratives around Palestine? How do you want to support Palestinian siblings?

CHAPER 14

A Vision for a Single State That Serves Both Jews and Palestinian Arabs in Equality

Jonathan Kuttab

The essence of the conflict between Zionism and Palestinian nationalism is again at the center of all events in Palestine/Israel. The idea of a two-state solution (basically dividing the land into a Jewish and an Arab state, along the 1967 lines) at one time gained a lot of international support. However, it has been thoroughly undermined by Jewish settlements being built in the 22 percent of the land that was supposed to serve as an Arab Palestinian state. Jewish Israelis seemed unwilling to allow for a truly independent Palestinian Arab state and continued to act as lords and sovereign in the occupied territories and use its resources on behalf of the Zionist project of serving Jews and Jews alone. Instead, the Zionist plan has been to keep control of the whole area of historic Palestine but to fragment the unity of Palestinian nationalism by forcibly dividing Palestinians into different populations (Palestinians who are Israeli citizens; East Jerusalemites; Gazans, West Bankers, and the refugees it had succeeded in removing from the area altogether). Yet this plan has not succeeded in obliterating the identity of Palestinian Arabs who still view themselves as one people. Similarly, the introduction of eight hundred thousand Jewish settlers into the West Bank, including East Jerusalem, was compounded by and has contributed to the strengthening of right-wing movements that insist on openly flaunting the Jewish character of the State of Israel at the expense of its Arab citizens (20 percent of the population). The message was clear to Palestinians: they would not be allowed a state in the West Bank/Gaza, and those of them who are citizens of Israel will not be allowed true equality as that state would be distinctly and exclusively Jewish.

The fact is that it is time to acknowledge that these two ideologies (an Israeli state as Jewish as France is French and Arab nationalism proclaiming that Palestine is Arab—*Falasteen Arabiyyeh*) are mutually exclusive, and each views the other as an existential threat. In their extreme versions, both groups are caught in a zero-sum situation, each claiming all the land for its own community and each viewing the other as illegitimate. Zionists would be eager to clear the land of all Arabs so that it is exclusively inhabited by Jews, tolerating non-Jews reluctantly only as long as they accept and acknowledge Jewish supremacy and domination. On the other hand, Palestinians view the Zionists as settler colonialists who are strangers and occupiers. Dividing the land along the 1967 borders may have been a pragmatic compromise, but it has been thoroughly undermined by the settler movement, both on the ground and at the theoretical level as Israeli policies and laws—and the settlers—consider themselves and their settlement homes and lands to be an integral part of the Jewish state, which they are not willing to turn over to Arab control. Dividing the land also perpetuates a zero-sum thinking where each side benefits only as the other side loses and where every advantage to one side necessarily detracts from the other.

Separation is neither a normal nor a healthy situation, especially since members of each community have valuable property, residences, connections, claims, and rights in the area scheduled to belong to the other side and can face discrimination and persecution in the part dedicated to that other side. Palestinian Arabs would still yearn for their homes in what is to be a Jewish state, and Arab citizens of Israel will feel left out of a solution that recognizes Israel as a Jewish state (where they are 20 percent of the population). Similarly, Jewish Israelis may feel an attachment to East Jerusalem and Hebron and other areas of what they call Judea and Samaria (the West Bank) for religious and historical reasons, and settlers may be unwilling to leave their settlements or to live under Arab rule.

The time, therefore, has come to think out of the box and to seek solutions that do not just try to balance the interests of the two ideologies, but to seek radical solutions, which may require adjustments of the two ideologies to take into account the interest of the other group. Zionists can no longer pretend that the land was empty, or that Palestinians are not a people, or that somehow Palestinians can be spirited away, forced out, or convinced to live in permanent subjugation in a system of apartheid, discrimination, and repression or, at best, as second-class residents in a country that is not theirs. Jewish Israelis need to adjust their Zionist ideology to take into account the indigenous Palestinian population that continues to live in the land and is going nowhere. Their "Jewish state" now has within it and under its control seven million non-Jews who need to be accommodated.

By the same token, Palestinians must understand that, however unjust, and whatever their own legitimate claims are, there are seven million Israeli Jews living in their land and they view as home and are here to stay. Palestinians therefore need to adjust their nationalism and national aspirations to take that fact into account.

A two-state solution based on dividing the land leaves the essential conflict in place as a valuable portion of the "homeland" would come outside the control of each party. This means that a solution based on ideologies of exclusive national claims and national identity will always perpetuate the conflict and will never satisfy either party. A two-state solution does not address this reality, and more people are increasingly willing to accept the reality of one state in all the land, and instead seek equality and rights for everyone within that state. Perhaps it is better to seek solutions or frameworks that address the true needs of the people on both sides.

Without pretending there is any symmetry between the two groups, and without arguing about the legitimacy of the claims of either, there needs to be a way to accommodate the actual interests of both groups. This is where a rights-based approach that seeks equality and satisfaction to both groups provides a way forward.

I have tried to envision such a solution in my book *Beyond the Two-State Solution*. I begin by listing the advantages that each ideology claimed to provide to its adherents, as well as the basic nonnegotiable needs of each group, and sought to address those needs and provide those advantages in a single state that serves the interests of both groups, without making any exclusivist claims for either party. In other words, the state can be both Jewish and Palestinian Arab without negating the national and personal claims of each group.

Under such a scheme, the state and its public institutions are required to serve all citizens on the basis of equality, rather than seek the advantage of one group or nationality at the expense of all others. No one would be forced to leave their current homes or lands they are currently cultivating or have built upon, even where it is clear they originally belonged to someone else. Compensation from public land and alternative housing would be provided instead to the original owner.

A democratic state that provides basic rights to all individuals and substantial minorities can be fully embraced by both groups. The basic concept is to provide rights to all and prevent a numerical majority for oppressing or delegitimizing the rights of a minority simply because they won the last election. This is based on firm guarantees in a constitution, with iron-clad requirements to respect the rights of the individual and of any minority. Institutions can be set in place to safeguard the interests of each group and to ensure that their basic rights are not infringed. An independent judiciary and a constitutional court, as well as a free press and a robust democracy, will constrain populism and ensure true liberty. There is a false view of democracy as a dictatorship by 51 percent of the electorate. Under such a view, each group would be obsessed with demography and fear every shift in demographic numbers. Under a true democracy, however, demography is not determinative, as each group is protected and supermajorities are required to alter the constitution or the carefully crafted structures that protect the individual and minorities from the vagaries of the electoral majorities.

For example, such a state would constitutionally recognize the right of return for all Jews, which is a basic tenant of Zionism, but it would equally protect the right of return ("*Awda*" in Arabic) for all Palestinian Arabs and their descendants. An appropriate governmental ministry would work for their absorption and accommodation. No Jewish settler (in Israel or the occupied territories) would be forced out of their homes, however they came to live there, but the original Palestinian owner would be compensated from public lands and funds with equivalent housing or land. In this way the new government would provide a measure of relative justice to all and avoid the bitterness and continued conflict that would result from the feeling of injustice and oppression. At the same time it would acknowledge the current realities on the ground without getting into disputes and arguments over the historical injustices that brought about that reality.

Pluralistic societies do exist in the world today, including the United States and Canada. And while tensions may exist—and racism and discrimination will need to be constantly and vigorously resisted—a legal framework can be imagined that would safeguard the rights of all. Structures can be created that would enable individuals and communities to challenge and end any systematic or public manifestations of inequality.

There are also unique aspects of the situation in Israel/Palestine that need to be addressed. The centrality of the land for people of all three monotheistic religions should be acknowledged, and religious freedoms and holy places should be protected. By the same token, civil courts should exist parallel to the religious courts to ensure the religious freedom of all religious denominations, as well as freedom of religion for those who chose to be free from the strictures of their own denomination or those who are secular or have mixed marriages. These are freedoms that do not exist today in Israel where, for Jews, only Orthodox rabbinical courts are allowed, with exclusive control over all Jews, including the Conservative, Reform and secular Jews; or in the Palestinian Territories, which also continue to be ruled by the Ottoman framework of *Millets* (communities), according exclusive authority in personal status matters to the religious community to which one belongs.

By concentrating on personal and communal rights and abandoning exclusive claims over all the land, both Jewish Israelis and Palestinian Arabs can live with freedom and dignity and democracy in a single state that is both Jewish and Arab, but not exclusively one or the other.

DISCUSSION QUESTIONS

1. Many global ethnic/tribal/religious conflicts have been ended by dividing the warring populations into their own separate states or enclaves (e.g., Ireland, Bosnia, Cameroon, and other post-colonial states). Do you think this has been successful, or do you agree with Mr. Kuttab that these types of divisions perpetuate a zero-sum thinking?

2. Many of our Palestinian partners have differing opinions about the viability of a two-state solution in Israel/Palestine. What do you think? Which argument is more compelling to you?

3. Many of our Palestinian partners have written in this book about the importance Palestinians place on their ties to the land. Mr. Kuttab argues for abandoning exclusive claims over all the land. Do you see these two arguments as complementary or in opposition to each other? Can one both have deep ties to the land and abandon exclusive claims?

CHAPTER 15

Pursuing Justice and a Just Peace

Rifat Kassis

At the heart of the Palestinian struggle for freedom, independence, and self-determination lies a profound aspiration for justice and a just peace. Understanding the significance of justice for Palestinians necessitates acknowledging the decades-long historical injustices they have endured. From systematic ethnic cleansing to relentless dispossession and oppressive control, Palestinians have faced unyielding atrocities at the hands of the Zionist movement and Israel for around a century, enduring direct military occupation for more than five decades.

These injustices have left a profound impact on Palestinian lives, shaping their daily realities and undermining their pursuit of freedom and dignity. Moreover, amidst these struggles, misconceptions persist about the history and current state of the Palestinian cause, hindering accurate understanding and perpetuating misconceptions. It is imperative to highlight the importance of dispelling these misunderstandings, as accurate understanding is essential to effectively address the ongoing plights faced by Palestinians and foster genuine efforts toward justice and self-determination. Some of these misunderstandings are rooted in the following misconceptions.

The Misleading Conception of the "Israeli-Palestinian Conflict"

Confusion often arises regarding the situation in Israel and Palestine, commonly referred to as the "Israeli-Palestinian conflict" by Western public officials, the media, and commentators. However, this terminology fails to capture the asymmetrical power dynamics and the root cause of colonization.

The Palestinians suffer under foreign brutal military occupation by Israel and systematic forcible displacement policies and practices including the installment of permit regimes, land annexation, denial of access to natural resources and services, discriminatory zoning and planning, denial of residency, expansion of settlements, and suppression of Palestinian resistance and culture. This in turn controls the lives and basic rights of Palestinians all over the fragmented territories including the Gaza Strip, the West Bank with East Jerusalem, as well as the Palestinian population with Israeli citizenship and the Palestinian refugees who are scattered worldwide.

Israel also denies Palestinian refugees and internally displaced persons from returning to their homes and cities, as mandated in UN Resolution 194 and international law. Thus, the issue is one of colonization, military occupation, and apartheid imposed by a foreign nation upon indigenous Palestinians.

Not Temporary Occupation, but Settler Colonization and an Apartheid System

The Palestinian plight extends beyond mere military occupation, representing a comprehensive system of settler colonization and apartheid. This system, characterized by legal, political, economic, cultural, and psychological structures, perpetuates institutionalized violence and discrimination against Palestinians. Practices such as checkpoints, settler attacks, and ongoing wars, including the genocidal war on Gaza, aim to demoralize and control the Palestinian population. The goal of these practices is clear: to annex a maximum amount of land with the least number of Palestinians, breaking their spirit and ensuring their subjugation. Israel's arbitrary and unchecked arrest and detention policies send a chilling message: resistance is futile, and Palestinians are deemed worthless and unprotected.

Israeli Overuse and Misuse of the Concepts of "Security," "Self-Defense," and Antisemitism

Israel employs the discourse of "state security" to justify its oppressive practices in the occupied Palestinian territory, labeling Palestinians as "security threats" or "terrorists." This narrative, cloaked in a veneer of (il-)legality through military orders and the vagueness of the terrorism definition on a global level, has persuaded both domestic and international audiences of the necessity of Israel's policies, granting it impunity for human rights abuses. In fact, Israel's definition of "security threat" is broad and materializes in a highly controversial law of the Israeli anti-terrorism law of 2016 that strangles the Palestinians' daily lives.

Moreover, based on numerous international law experts as well the International Court of Justice Advisory Opinion on the Wall in 2004, Israel does not have the right to claim the right of self-defense against a threat that emanates from the territory it occupies and has kept under belligerent occupation for more than five decades coupled with an inhumane siege for around two decades. Israel, as an occupying power, continues to have the obligation to protect the population it occupies, even after such attacks.

Furthermore, as for the Israeli weaponization of anti-Zionism, any critique of Israel or the Zionist movement is strategically labeled as antisemitism, stifling legitimate dissent, solidarity, and resistance efforts. One of the tools employed by Israel in this regard is the heavily criticized International Holocaust Remembrance Alliance working definition, where seven of the eleven examples included in the definition center around criticizing Israel as a state. The problem is that this definition is being adopted by Western states and implemented throughout the institutions of these countries. Therefore, any criticism of Israel is branded by definition as racism and antisemitism.

The Fallacy of Blaming Solely the Israeli Governments without Recognizing Zionism as the Root Cause to Displacement and Dispossession

While much scrutiny rightly falls upon the actions and policies of consecutive Israeli governments, it is crucial to recognize that the root of the problem lies within the broader colonial Zionist project and ideology. This misconception obscures the deeper historical and systemic injustices faced by Palestinians, which extend far beyond the purview of this government or that. In this context, many oppressive and racist laws such as Israel's Nation State Law of 2018 and the wider criminalization of human rights organizations have been developed and enacted during so-called centrist governments while settlement building and expansion have continued under every Israeli government.

Zionism -as a violent, colonial, and supremacist project and ideology dating back over a century- aimed at the establishment of a Jewish homeland, exclusively for Jews, in mandate Palestine, a geographical area predominantly inhabited by non-Jewish people, resulting in the displacement, dispossession, and marginalization of the indigenous Palestinian population.

This colonial mindset, ingrained in the fabric of Israeli society, perpetuates structural inequality and oppression, affecting all aspects of Palestinian life. Therefore, addressing the complexities of the Palestinian struggle requires a deeper understanding of the historical, ideological, and systemic factors at play, moving beyond mere governmental critique to challenge the very foundations of colonialism and ethno-nationalism in the region.

The Entrenched Apparatus of Injustice

Keeping the aforementioned points in mind, one is better equipped to understand and conceptualize the historical events of 1947–1948, when over 580 Palestinian villages were destroyed and depopulated with more than 750,000 Palestinians forcibly displaced from their homeland, consecutively resulting in the establishment of the State of Israel. These events initiated decades of ethnic cleansing, settler colonial military occupation, and an apartheid system over the Palestinians. As a result, Palestinians suffered fragmentation and segregation, as most Palestinians became refugees scattered around the world. In this context, the West Bank fell under the administration of Jordan, the Gaza Strip under Egyptian administration, and those who remained in Israel proper were classified as second-class citizens in their own homeland.

Moreover, a military occupation system was formally established in 1967, and the apparatus of injustice grew increasingly entrenched and complex. Today the Israeli occupation continues to provide security and services for more than nine hundred thousand illegal settlers, half of whom are heavily armed, residing in Jewish-only settlements on Palestinian lands confiscated by Israel in the West Bank, including East Jerusalem.

Around three million Palestinians living in the West Bank are subject to a system of collective punishment and apartheid, with severe limitations on access to basic services and rights. Palestinians also face continuous Israeli attempts to demographically reengineer the West Bank through frequent demolishing of Palestinian homes, construction of settler-exclusive roads, and construction of a separation wall extending over seven hundred kilometers in the West Bank. This all has resulted in economic, social, educational, and political stranglehold on Palestinian communities, creating a coercive environment that forces Palestinians to leave their lands.

The situation in Jerusalem has become increasingly volatile, where Palestinians confront forced evictions, house demolitions, ID card revocations, denial of family unification, and settlement constructions within their neighborhoods, with the Israeli government threatening to divide al-Aqsa Mosque, exacerbating tensions and downgrading a political struggle into a religious conflict.

Moreover, thousands of Palestinian political prisoners, including women and children, are currently detained, with numbers skyrocketing since the onset of the genocidal war on Gaza in October 2023. These prisoners endure physical and psychological abuse, torture, and violations of their legal and human rights. Palestinians in the occupied Palestinian territories face severe restrictions on movement, limited access to employment, health care, places of worship, and educational institutions, as well as frequent humiliations and arbitrary arrests.

Today, as we all witness the unfolding genocide in Gaza, it is crucial to highlight the physical and emotional devastation wrought by Israel's sixteen-year siege of Gaza. More than 110,000 people have been killed, injured, or trapped under rubble in the quickest killing rate seen in decades. Approximately 70 percent of buildings and infrastructure, including schools, universities, hospitals, and places of worship, have been partially or completely destroyed.

Almost all Palestinians in Gaza have been affected, with hundreds of thousands displaced to shelters and open land. Food, water, electricity, and fuel supplies have been completely cut off by Israel.[36] Israel is furthermore crippling and limiting the distribution of aid in Gaza and is using food as a war tactic to purposely starve the population. In this light, Israel is trying to delegitimize the United Nations Relief and Works Agency (UNRWA) as the largest and most crucial aid provider in Gaza and is pressurizing major donor-states to cut off their aid to the agency.

What future awaits Gaza after such destruction?

Pursuing Justice

Since the signing of the Declaration of Principles between Israel and the Palestinian Liberation Organization in 1993, both parties have engaged in a so-called peace process that has yielded no tangible results for Palestinians and has ultimately failed to deliver peace. Israel has consistently displayed a lack of interest in reaching an agreement that offers any semblance of dignity or justice to the Palestinians.

Therefore, at the core of the Palestinian quest for justice and self-determination lies the demand for the dismantlement of the colonial-apartheid system imposed on Palestinians wherever they reside and the immediate cessation of all manifestations of Israeli occupation of Palestinians and Palestinian territory.

Additionally, justice entails the realization of the right of Palestinian refugees and their offspring to return to their ancestral homes from which they were forcibly expelled during the *Nakba* in 1948 and to receive compensation for the suffering they endured. This

---

[36] UN Office of the High Commissioner for Human Rights "Over one hundred days into the war, Israel destroying Gaza's food system and weaponizing food, say UN human rights experts" January 16, 2024, https://www.ohchr.org/en/press-releases/2024/01/over-one-hundred-days-war-israel-destroying-gazas-food-system-and

right, enshrined in UN General Assembly Resolution 194, represents a fundamental principle of justice and redress for the injustices suffered by Palestinians.

Another crucial aspect of justice for Palestinians is the pursuit of self-determination, which includes the right to equality and nondiscrimination. Palestinians aspire to live in a society where they enjoy equal rights and opportunities, regardless of their ethnicity, religion, or nationality. This includes access to education, health care, employment, and political participation without facing discrimination or marginalization. However, the reality on the ground paints a different picture. Palestinians living under Israeli rule, whether in the occupied Palestinian territories or within the green line, face systemic discrimination and inequality in all aspects of life.

Justice for Palestinians also requires accountability for human rights violations and crimes committed against them by holding perpetrators accountable through fair and impartial judicial processes, prosecuting those responsible for war crimes, crimes against humanity and genocide, as well as providing redress and reparations to victims and their families. Moreover, justice must be accompanied by genuine efforts towards truth, reconciliation, and healing.

Central to the Palestinian quest for justice is the realization of their right to freedom and sovereignty. Palestinians aspire to establish an independent and viable state of their own. Yet the continued occupation and colonization of Palestinian territories have undermined the prospects for a two-state solution. Israeli policies and practices in the occupied Palestinian territories made the establishment of a contiguous and sovereign Palestinian state increasingly challenging. Today many Palestinians believe a single democratic state for all its citizens may be the only viable option to achieve justice and a realistic, humane solution for all peoples living in historical Palestine.

Finally, justice for Palestinians entails recognition of their national identity as well as acknowledgment of the Palestinian people's cultural, historical, and political aspirations, affirming their right to resist, exist, and thrive as a distinct national community.

Toward a Just Peace

In conclusion, justice and just peace stand as fundamental aspirations of the Palestinian people, deeply rooted in their historical experiences of oppression and resistance. To achieve justice, it is imperative to address the root causes of the situation, including settler colonization, apartheid, military occupation, and the dispossession of Palestinian land and rights. This endeavor necessitates a steadfast commitment to equality, accountability, sovereignty, and the inherent dignity and rights of all Palestinians.

This commitment can be shown by Israel and its Western allies through acknowledging the ongoing *nakba* of the Palestinian people as a start. However, to this day they persist in not only denying Palestinians their right to self-determination and return, which further perpetuate the *nakba* which Palestinians continue to endure, but they are also accused of committing, being complicit in, and enabling a genocide against the Palestinian people.

It is therefore evident that only by adhering to international law embedded within principles of justice through genuine international efforts towards a just peace that perceives Palestinians as rights holders and respects their struggle for liberty can the Palestinian people realize their long-awaited liberation and fulfill their aspirations for a future defined by dignity, freedom, and self-determination. The time for echoing empty statements is long over; now is the time for action.

DISCUSSION QUESTIONS

1. Do you think the vision of a future of just peace for Palestinians laid out by Mr. Kassis differs from the ones suggested by Mr. Kuttab or Rev. Dr. Ateek in previous chapters? If so, how? What are the similarities?

2. Where around the world do you think there has been success in achieving truth and reconciliation post-conflict? Where do you see steps toward a just peace?

CHAPTER 16

Economic Measures in the Pursuit of Justice

Krista Johnson Weicksel

Let each of you look not to your own interests but to the interests of others.

Philippians 2:4 (NRSVUE)

If our madness could end as it did, it must be possible to do the same everywhere else in the world. If peace could come to South Africa, surely it can come to the Holy Land.

Archbishop Desmond Tutu

In 2005, Palestinian civil society called for Boycott, Divestment and Sanctions against Israel until it complies with international law and universal principles of human rights. The call stated:

We, representatives of Palestinian civil society, call upon international civil society organizations and people of conscience all over the world to impose broad boycotts and implement divestment initiatives against Israel similar to those applied to South Africa in the apartheid era. We appeal to you to pressure your respective states to impose embargoes and sanctions against Israel. We also invite conscientious Israelis to support this Call, for the sake of justice and genuine peace.

Three UCC and Disciples partners endorsed the call: the YWCA of Palestine, the East Jerusalem YMCA, and the Middle East Council of Churches Department of Service to Palestinian Refugees' Gaza Committee.

This campaign has encouraged use of these measures to pressure Israel to recognize the Palestinian people's right to self-determination, end the occupation, recognize the rights of Arab-Palestinian citizens of Israel to full equality, and recognize the right of return for Palestinian refugees.

In 2005 the General Synod of the United Church of Christ adopted a resolution titled "Concerning Use of Economic Leverage in Promoting Peace in the Middle East." This resolution called upon UCC settings and members

> to use economic leverage, including, but not limited to: advocating the reallocation of US foreign aid so that the militarization of the Middle East is constrained; making positive contributions to groups and partners committed to the non-violent resolution of the conflict; challenging the practices of corporations that gain from the continuation of the conflict; and divesting from those companies that refuse to change their practices of gain from the perpetuation of violence, including the Occupation.

In 2015 the General Synod of the United Church of Christ adopted a resolution titled "A Call for the United Church of Christ to Take Actions Toward a Just Peace in the Israeli-Palestinian Conflict." This resolution called upon members of the UCC to "boycott goods identified as being produced in or using the facilities of illegal settlements located in the Occupied Palestinian Territories." Likewise, the 2021 "Compelled to Witness" letter released by leaders of the Christian Church (Disciples of Christ) and the subsequent 2023 resolution of the same name said: "We support the use of economic measures to hold countries and companies accountable to standards of human rights and national and international laws. We oppose efforts to criminalize them in states and provinces, and nationally."

There have been efforts to criminalize Boycott, Divestment, and Sanctions efforts. In the past ten years thirty-eight U.S. states have passed some form of legislation targeting boycotts for Palestinian rights.

This ranges from prohibitions on state contracts with individuals or organizations that support boycotts to requiring contractors to sign contracts pledging they will not boycott Israel. The Israel Anti-Boycott Act, which has been introduced in Congress several times, would impose criminal penalties for the support of these economic measures.

The use of economic measures is one tool of nonviolent resistance. During apartheid in South Africa, South African civil society called for the use of boycott, divestment, and sanctions against South Africa. When apartheid did end, it was believed that the use of economic measures had played a role in that change. It should be said that the call from Palestinian civil society does differ in notable ways from the South African context. In South Africa the majority of the South African population was calling for these boycotts and sanctions upon their own government, with a formal call from the African National Congress and endorsement from the UN. In Israel/Palestine the boycott, divestment, and sanctions call originated from Palestinian civil society. The Palestinian Joint Advocacy Initiative said in a statement: "The main hurdle facing civil society's efforts to compel Israel to end its brutal policies against the Palestinians is the fact that such efforts are neither centralized nor emanate from a well-regarded Palestinian source of authority and leadership."

Churches were involved in the anti-Apartheid struggle, and some employed boycotts and divestment. Other examples of instances where churches have used economic measures to seek justice include:

- Support for the Coalition of Immokalee Workers to seek fair wages for farm workers who pick tomatoes used by major restaurant chains. The churches have affirmed boycotts of Taco Bell and Wendy's in support of the farm workers;

- Support for the Farm Labor Organizing Committee in the boycott of Mt. Olive Pickle Company to seek better wages for those who pick cucumbers;

- Support for United Farm Workers in grape and lettuce boycotts aimed at securing fair wages for farm workers;

- Opposition to the use of racially offensive names and logos by professional sports teams through boycotts;

- Participation in the Interfaith Center for Corporate Responsibility to promote socially responsible practices by various companies through shareholder activism;

- Corporate engagement with and/or divestment from fossil fuel companies in the context of the climate change debates.

In practice, employing economic measures may change an individual's shopping practice at the grocery store by choosing to buy a generic brand of hummus instead of the Sabra brand hummus, which has been known to make financial contributions to portions of the Israel Defense Forces. Individuals, congregations, and conferences/regions can research where their investments are held and ask if those portfolios include companies that profit from the Israeli occupation, applying a social screen that would prevent such investments. It may also include direct advocacy calling on companies to make a change and encouraging consumer boycott until a company changes its practices.

In 2020 the UCC joined the "No Dough for Occupation" campaign focused on Pillsbury products made in a facility in an illegal Israeli settlement in occupied East Jerusalem. General Mills, the parent company of Pillsbury headquartered in Minnesota, had built a factory on land that Israel had illegally confiscated from the Palestinian neighborhood of Beit Hanina in East Jerusalem. Israeli settlements in the Occupied Palestinian Territories are illegal under international law. Most Israeli settlements are residential, but there are several areas which are industrial, including the Atarot Industrial Zone in East Jerusalem, the settlement where General Mills had a factory producing Pillsbury products. Companies that do business in illegal settlements profit from unjust systems and do so despite international law.

Charlie Pillsbury, a UCC church member and a member of the Pillsbury family, whose ancestor Charles Pillsbury founded the Pillsbury Company over 150 years ago, wrote an April 2021 op-ed on behalf of many members of his family in the *Minneapolis Star Tribune*. It said:

We take pride in seeing our family name associated with products sold around the world. But in these times we no longer can in good conscience buy products bearing our name. ... As long as General Mills continues to profit from the dispossession and suffering of the Palestinian people, we will not buy any Pillsbury products. We call on General Mills to stop doing business on occupied land. And we call on people of good conscience and all socially responsible organizations across the globe to join in boycotting Pillsbury products until General Mills stops this illegal and immoral practice.

In June 2022 General Mills announced it had divested its Israeli business and ended the production of Pillsbury products in an illegal settlement. In response, the American Friends Service Committee, initiator of the No Dough for Occupation campaign, said, "This victory shows that public pressure works, even on the largest of corporations."

Other consumer boycotts are targeted at PayPal, HP, and Airbnb. PayPal has refused, so far, to contract with Palestinian businesses and banks in the West Bank or Gaza. It does, however, work with Israeli banks, allowing businesses located in the illegal Israeli settlements in the West Bank to benefit from PayPal's services. Palestinians are unable to establish bank accounts in Israeli banks and are therefore excluded.

HP is a major contractor for the Israeli Ministry of Defense and knowingly supports Israel's occupation of Palestinian land. HP supplies the biometric equipment Israel uses at military checkpoints in the occupied West Bank to track and restrict the movement of Palestinians.

Airbnb allows listing of rental properties in illegal Israeli settlements in the West Bank. In 2018 the company said it would remove those listings then quickly reversed that decision following a number of lawsuits. Airbnb claims to donate the profit it generates through these listings, but allowing them to remain in place means that a wider tourist industry is being supported and allowed to flourish at the expense of Palestinian rights and livelihoods.

Knowing what you own is the first step to aligning your investments with your values. You may be invested in state violence through companies involved in the Israeli military occupation. The American Friends Service Committee Investigate Project database (investigate.afsc.org) includes original research and lists over two hundred company profiles. You can search the database for a specific company or investment fund. Learn how they profit from and support state violence, then use this knowledge to create change.

DISCUSSION QUESTIONS

1. This chapter outlines the success of using economic measures in helping to end the apartheid era in South Africa. Can you think of other successful boycott, divestment, or sanctions campaigns? Can you think of unsuccessful campaigns?

2. Do you think the Palestinian Boycott, Divestment, and Sanctions movement has had any success?

3. Would you be willing to engage in economic measures including boycott and divestment? Why or why not?

4. There is a saying that the money you spend reflects your values. What values appear on your last bank statement? How can you align your spending to better match your values?

Easter Amidst a Genocide

Rev. Dr. Munther Isaac

This chapter is adapted from a sermon delivered on Holy Saturday evening during a virtual Easter vigil for Gaza on March 30, 2024. You can watch this sermon on YouTube.[37]

Palestinians celebrated Easter in Palestine in 2024 in the most difficult circumstance. Easter week coincided with 170 days since the genocide in Gaza began. At the time, the war had entered a new phase, in which Gazans were being killed by hunger, thirst, and disease. They were starved to death. It was a slow death. Gazans were hanging between heaven and earth, dying slowly, while the world was watching. They have "no form or majesty" that we should look at them ... "from whom men hide their face."

A genocide has been normalized. As people of faith, if we truly claim to follow a crucified savior, we can never be ok with this. We should never accept the normalization of a genocide. We should never be ok with children dying from starvation, not because of drought or famine, but because of a manmade catastrophe! Because of the empire.

A genocide has been normalized just as apartheid was normalized in Palestine and before that in South Africa. Just as slavery and the caste system were normalized. It has been firmly established to us that the leaders of the super powers and those who benefit from this modern colonialism do not look at us as equals. They created a narrative to normalize genocide. They have a theology for it. A genocide has been normalized. This is racism at its worst.

The very same political and church leaders who lined up in October one after the other to give the green line for this genocide,

[37] https://www.globalministries.org/a-palestinian-christian-reflection-on-the-meaning-of-easter/

giving it the cover of "self-defense," cannot even bring themselves to condemn the obvious war crimes being committed by Israel. They are good at raising their concern. Making statements that they are "troubled" by the killing of our children. They want to convince us that they care. They raise funds. They are silent during the genocide, and then show up afterwards, with charity, to say that they care. Can we really accept this?

Many countries rushed to suspend their funding of UNRWA [the United Nations Relief and Works Agency] based on mere allegations that were not fully proven, yet did nothing with regards to the clear findings of the ICJ [International Court of Justice]. The amount of hypocrisy is incomprehensible. The level of racism involved for such hypocrisy is appalling.

Now some politicians claim that their patience with Israel is ending—and we say: Nothing can wash the blood from your hands. The UN Security Council resolution [in March 2024 that called for a ceasefire] was way too late. It means nothing. Some acted as if we should congratulate or thank the USA for not vetoing the resolution. I say: Absolutely not. They are complicit. You cannot undo the past. In fact, the U.S. has just sent another massive missile package to arm Israel. Are they really trying to fool us? Claiming that they care, and that they are concerned. If the flow of U.S. weapons stops, the war would end within days. Instead, they send Israel missiles to kill us, and then send a fraction of the needed food parcels. This is beyond complicit. This is direct involvement in this genocide.

In This Easter, We Turn First to the Cross

We are mourning. These are dark, dark days. In times like this, we Palestinians look at the cross, identify with the cross, and see Jesus identifying with us. The cross is an important Palestinian symbol.

During Easter we relive his arrest, torture, and execution at the hands of Empire—with the complicity of a religious ideology of course. In the Easter story, we find comfort and empowerment in knowing that Jesus identifies with us.

During Christmastime our church created a special manger of Christ under the rubble. At the time I said if Jesus were born in our world today, he would be born under the rubble in Gaza, in solidarity with the children of Gaza and to identify with those suffering and marginalized.[38] We have kept the pile of rubble in our church since Christmas because Gaza is still under the rubble and because our people and our children in Gaza are still being pulled from under the rubble at this very moment.

I recently watched with anguish a cruel scene of a child pulled from under the rubble. He miraculously survived the bombing, and while he was being pulled out he was saying: "Where is the water? I am thirsty."

This reminded me of the words of Jesus on the cross, when he cried out: "I am thirsty." He cried out "I am thirsty" in solidarity with those being massacred by famine, siege, and bombardment. Jesus stands in solidarity with all the victims of wars and forced famines caused by unjust and tyrannical regimes in our world. It is the cry of everyone oppressed by the injustice of power and humanity's silence and inability to put an end to tyranny and injustice.

Jesus shouted, "I am thirsty," so they gave him vinegar to drink. They added more pain to his pain, more anguish to his anguish. Today, while Gaza screams, "I am thirsty," they drop aid from the sky, stained with the blood of innocents. Some were killed by drowning while trying to pull the dropped aid from the sea. How cruel. Gaza is thirsty, and they give Gaza vinegar.

We searched for God in this war. We cried out to him, and there was no answer, it seems, until we encountered the Son of God hanging on the cross, crying out: "My God, my God, why have you forsaken me?" Why did you let me be crucified? Alone? While I am innocent?

This is the cry of feeling abandoned. I am sure this is how Gazans feel today. Abandonment from the world leaders, not only Western, but also Arab and Muslim leaders abandoned us. Many in the church

---

[38] https://www.globalministries.org/christ-in-the-rubble-a-liturgy-of-lament-christmas-lutheran-church-bethlehem/

also watched from a distance, like Peter did when Jesus was arrested. Peter wanted to be safe; he lacked the courage ... similar to many church leaders today, who say one thing behind closed doors and another in public.

Yet it is in this cry—"My God, my God, why have you forsaken me?"—that we experience God, that God draws near to us, and it is in this cry that we feel his embrace and warmth. This is one of the mysteries of Easter.

In this land even God is a victim of oppression, death, the war machine, and colonialism. He suffers with the people of this land, sharing the same fate with them. "My God, my God, why have you forsaken me?" It is a cry that has resonated for years in this land. It is the cry of every oppressed person hanging in a state of slow death. It is a cry that Jesus shared with us in his pain, torment, and crucifixion. Today we place the cross on the rubble, remembering that Jesus shared the same fate with us, as he died on the cross as a victim of the colonizers.

And it became dark. The universe became dark in grief over the absence of truth. The universe became dark, lamenting the absence of justice. The cross is the ultimate injustice. Today the universe is saddened by the silence of decision-makers and their racism and by the silence of many who did not speak a word of truth, out of fear, armed with the theology of neutrality and inaction, under the banner of peace and reconciliation.

Today the universe became dark lamenting the apathy and numbness to suffering that exist in our world and the racism that led to normalizing and justifying a genocide.

What many in the church lack the most today is courage. They know the truth. But they are not speaking the truth because they fear the consequences. They fear the backlash! Many in the church want to avoid controversy. Can you imagine if Jesus walked on earth avoiding controversy! They write statements, and the way church statements dance around the issue of "ceasefire" or (God forbid) condemning Israel is indeed amazing. They write multi-page statements that basically say nothing other than unequivocally condemning October 7!

There are some church leaders who are willing to sacrifice us for comfort, the same way they offered us as an atonement sacrifice for their own racism and antisemitism—repenting on our land over a sin they committed in their land!

All of this while claiming to follow a crucified Savior, who sacrificed everything, endured pain and rejection for the sake of those he loved!

We of course must thank those who carried our cross with us. We really appreciate the demonstrations taking place for Gaza all over the world, as well as solidarity pilgrimages coming to visit us in these times. We thank those who came to Palestine to be in solidarity with us. We thank the doctors and nurses volunteering in Rafah. We thank those lobbying to stop weapon sales. We thank those demonstrating in the streets. We thank those who did many sit-ins and nonviolent protests. We thank those who keep disturbing the comfort of world leaders in gatherings and press conferences and fundraisers. We hear you! This is the church of Christ!

We salute those who resigned from government and international bodies in protest. They have courage and integrity. They understand that Gaza is indeed the moral compass of our world today.

We thank South Africa for its action in the ICJ and Algeria for leading the efforts for a ceasefire resolution. Both, by the way, survivors of colonialism! It is there where the moral credibility lies!

We are carrying a heavy cross. And our Friday has lasted way too long. But we know from the experience of Jesus that this suffering is not for the glorification of suffering. We know that suffering is always a path to glory and life. It is a stop on the road to resurrection. We walk with Jesus on the road to Golgotha. We are empowered by his solidarity with us, but we look for Sunday.

In Easter, We Turn to the Empty Tomb

What gave Jesus this strength? This resilience and power—to the extent that he forgave his oppressors? To the extent that he said, "Your will be done," and went voluntarily to the cross? I believe his resolve and determination—his resilience—came from trusting his Father's will and from knowing that his Father is able to raise him from the dead—and that he will ultimately do that! His faith sustained and empowered him. He was defiant in the face of empire; he faced the cross and even death with confidence and steadfastness.

I must admit: it is so difficult today to hold to our faith and to hope. We cannot see Sunday. It seems an impossibility. We are swallowed by the darkness of the tomb. Our strength has failed. We are weary.

It is so hard to speak of the resurrection now. We are mourning. Our siblings in Gaza are literally dying from starvation. But we *CANNOT* lose our faith in God. This is our last resort. As such, we have to fight to keep this faith. We cannot lose our faith. We have to look at the empty tomb. We must remember the empty tomb.

Today I preach to myself with the psalmist: "Why are you cast down, O my soul, and why are you in turmoil within me? Hope in God; for I shall again praise him, my salvation and my God."[39]

The Resurrection gives us hope. Christianity is a faith that hopes. Hope is not a denial of reality. We are not blind to our reality, and we as Palestinians realize the corruption and evil of the world—probably more than anybody else. But we must refuse to let this be the last word.

Christ is Risen—this is the final word. Christ is Risen, and this changes everything. The empty tomb is our hope. Behind the apartheid wall, and specifically in the Church of the Holy Sepulcher in Jerusalem, there is an empty tomb that reminds us that the last word is not that of death but of life. Not that of darkness but of light. Not that of genocide and starvation but of dignity and pride.

The empty tomb reminds us that evil, injustice, or tyranny cannot have the last word. If Christ had remained in his grave, Caesar and Pilate would have triumphed. Rome would have won and the Pharisees won. The oppressors would have been victorious. But Christ is Risen. The Empire is defeated—and, even better, death itself is defeated.

---

[39] Psalm 42:11

Because we have faith, we do not live in despair. Faith is the only thing they cannot take away from us.

When we declare on Easter Sunday, "a*l-maseeh qam*"—"Christ is Risen"—we declare that the final word belongs to God. We declare that justice is served. Truth is vindicated. The Empire and its allies lost. Today, after two thousand years, by continuing to carry the cross, we defeat and even mock the empire and its theology. We took the symbol of Rome's power and the means of its humiliation of others and made it the symbol of our strength, victory, and steadfastness in the face of death, and this is because a*l-maseeh qam*— Christ is Risen.

The Resurrection urges us to rise and act! Because we know that the final word belongs to God, we rise and act. We build. We preach love because we know love wins. We preach peace because peace wins. We preach life because death is defeated. Jesus stared death in the face and defeated it. And therefore, we rise and act.

Friends: I am confident that we the Palestinians will rise. Never in my life have I been prouder and more honored to be a Palestinian more than these last 175 days. I am proud of our resilience, *sumud*. I am proud of our solidarity with one another, our unity. When I say we will be ok and that we will recover, I say it because I know my people; I know who we are. Palestine is our homeland. We are deeply rooted here. For those Palestinians exiled around the world, Palestine lives in them. Palestine is in every corner of this earth. We will never relinquish our God-given rights of living in dignity and justice. Yet I also say we will recover because I believe in a good and just God who rules the world with justice. Probably our biggest asset is the justice of our cause. Our *sumud* ("steadfastness") is anchored in our just cause and our historical rootedness in this land, but also in this just nature of God. Because he lives, we can face all things, stare the empire in the face, and defeat it.

So today let the way of the cross be our way. Let the way of sacrificial love be our way. The crucified Jesus, who sacrificed his life for the sake of those he loved, calls us for costly solidarity, the costly solidarity of love. This is a call to action, for the church to be Jesus' church—to follow in the footsteps of our crucified savior.

The cross is God's solidarity with humanity in its pain and suffering, and God's solidarity must become our solidarity. The followers of Jesus risk all to speak truth to power. This is not about making a statement. Jesus did not say, "I was hungry, and you prayed for me and made a statement!" Jesus said, "I was a prisoner, and you came to me!" We must find ways to make a difference. We must act, mobilize, pressure, lobby, hold powers and leaders accountable. As people of the resurrection, we must unsettle the Empire. Today the land of the resurrection calls you to act in hope and love. Together we are committed to end this genocide. Together we are committed to work for truth and justice. We know we will prevail because al-maseeh qam. Christ is Risen. Amen.

DISCUSSION QUESTIONS

1. Rev. Dr. Isaac mentions that Palestinians identify with Jesus, particularly in the story of Easter. How do you identify with Jesus? Which story of Jesus resonates with you and your life?

2. Rev. Dr. Isaac highlights that Christians took the cross, a symbol of Empire and suffering, and reclaimed it as a symbol of strength, victory, and steadfastness. Where else have you seen symbols or words reclaimed by those oppressed by those symbols?

3. Reflect on this meditation. What challenged you? Where did you agree? What moved you?

Ways to Take Action

- Tell Congress to stop sending military aid to Israel. Research how your own members of Congress have voted on such bills, and reach out to make your voice heard. Participate in peaceful protests of U.S. military aid to Israel.
- Donate to UCC and Disciples partners in the region.
- Join the Apartheid-Free Campaign, and sign the Apartheid-Free pledge (apartheid-free.org).
- Look into your investments using the American Friends Service Committee Investigate tool (investigate.afsc.org), and see if your investments support state violence. Then make a choice whether you want to divest. Ask your employer and/or financial advisor about their investments, particularly any pension or other retirement plans.
- Include Palestinians and their experiences in your sermons and prayers. Lift Palestine, Israel, and their leaders and citizens in your individual prayers often.
- Support a child's education in Palestine through Global Ministries' Child & Elder Sponsorship Program (globalministries.org/child_sponsorship).
- Travel responsibly. Join a People to People Pilgrimage or other opportunity provided by our partners and visit Palestinians, not just biblical or historical sites.

Appendix A

The Disciples and UCC and the Middle East through Assembly and Synod Positions

Dr. Peter Makari

The Christian Church (Disciples of Christ) and United Church of Christ have extensively developed positions on Israel/Palestine expressed by their respective churchwide governing bodies, the General Assembly and General Synod. These bodies speak to, but not for, the churches. The positions form the guidance and parameters to which the national or general ministry settings of the two churches refer when offering public witness on the issue and are an expression of the church's attentiveness to the changing realities in the region. These positions are how the church as a larger whole communicates to the world—including to their own members and to partners in the region—our continued deep engagement. Resolutions adopted by the General Assembly and General Synod are informed primarily by the voices of our partners in the region. Through these partnerships, the Disciples and UCC have access to perspectives that are not as commonly available through commercial media. Our churches' positions are also impacted by the presence and perspectives of mission personnel who serve at the invitation of partners. They are further influenced by members of our churches who are committed to raising a voice of peace and justice for the region, often resulting from firsthand experience they have had by travel and encounter.

The form and format of resolutions have changed over the years, with a more developed text being required in recent years. Early resolutions are therefore less extensive or substantive, but this does not diminish their force. It is significant that both churches have engaged the issues related to Israel/Palestine in similar, but not always parallel, ways, and have done so since the early years in the modern manifestations in the lives of the two denominations. The UCC, established in 1957, first spoke on Israel/Palestine at its fifth General Synod in 1967, mere weeks after the 1967 War, when it spoke on the need for a "just treatment for Palestinian refugees and relief of their suffering."[40] The Disciples of Christ, having implemented "The Design"—effectively the constitution of the church—in 1968, first spoke on the Middle East in 1973, when it addressed the United Nations' peacekeeping role, also just a few short weeks after the 1973 War, another major war in the region.

In the first years of General Synod, the UCC focused primarily on increasing awareness about the situation in the Middle East, as well as on supporting partners in responding to the needs of refugees and supporting U.S. government efforts to minimize tensions in the region, especially in light of the Cold War between the U.S. and the USSR, in which the Middle East was a theatre of engagement. Very early on, in 1973, the UCC affirmed the rights of Israel and the Palestinian Arabs as a way to achieving peace and security and cautioned against the weaponization of the actors.

By the end of the 1970s and early 1980s, both churches, as members of the National Council of Churches of Christ in the USA, were supportive of the NCC's Policy Statement on the Middle East, which supported, among other things, the rights of Israelis and Palestinians to security and peace within recognized borders and a shared Jerusalem open to Israelis and Palestinians—Jews, Christians, and Muslims alike. The UCC had also adopted a resolution in 1979 that welcomed the Camp David Accords signed between Egypt and Israel. In 1983 the Disciples adopted a resolution expressing concern over the proliferation of arms in the region, and the UCC in 1989 called on governments to eliminate further military aid or intervention in the region.

---

[40] "Resolution on the Middle East Situation" General Synod 5, 1967, https://uccresolutions.org/wp-content/uploads/2023/06/67-GS-94.pdf

In 1993 both churches adopted resolutions urging the reopening of the city of Jerusalem, following a ban on access that Israel had imposed, and in 1997 both churches again spoke in one voice adopting parallel resolutions titled "Jerusalem: City of Life," which recognized the importance of the city for all three Abrahamic faiths, urged that it be a city at peace and recognized as the capital for both Israel and the Palestinians, and that negotiators move beyond exclusivist claims to create a Jerusalem that would be a "sign of peace and symbol of reconciliation for all humankind."

In the late 1990s and early 2000s the language of adopted resolutions became increasingly critical of the ongoing occupation, including condemnation of Israeli settlement construction and expansion, while also calling for the building of Palestinian infrastructure. The UCC, concerned about the proliferation and influence of Christian Zionism, passed a resolution focusing attention on the theology and offering an alternative voice.

In 2005 both churches adopted resolutions calling for the elimination of Israel's separation barrier due to its route, which encroaches on Palestinian lands in the West Bank occupied since 1967, separating Palestinians from their land and each other, and for theological reasons as a barrier to peace. The 2005 Assembly also adopted a resolution condemning suicide bombings by Palestinians, consistent with the Disciples opposition to violence.

The 2005 General Synod was also significant for the UCC in that a landmark resolution calling for the use of economic measures to promote peace was adopted. The resolution called for advocacy to reallocate U.S. foreign aid so that the militarization of the Middle East is constrained; positive contributions to groups and partners committed to the nonviolent resolution of the conflict; challenging the practices of corporations that gain from the continuation of the conflict; and divesting from those companies that refuse to change their practices of gain from the perpetuation of violence. It was only the second denomination in the U.S. to endorse such a strategy. This was followed in 2015 with a further resolution that called the UCC to action to promote a just peace in the Israeli-Palestinian conflict.

That resolution identified a strategy for the UCC that combined: educational empowerment; economic leverage, including divestment and boycotts; political pressure and advocacy with U.S. elected officials; and interreligious dialogue with Jews and Muslims.

The Disciples of Christ Assembly in 2013, recognizing that church groups often travel to the region to visit the places of the biblical story, adopted a resolution calling on church members to seek a fuller experience that would include visiting church partners and mission coworkers and to understand the current reality and context through their eyes.

In 2017 the Disciples and UCC adopted parallel resolutions affirming the rights of children living under Israeli occupation. The resolution included advocacy for the human rights of children, identifying the traumatic situation of children living with constant fear of arrest, detention, and violence; insisting that Palestinian children be treated in accordance with international juvenile justice standards, specifically the United Nations Convention on the Rights of the Child; calling the United States government to adhere to U.S. laws concerning human rights violations and the disbursement of military aid and assistance to Israeli armed forces; and urging the United States Senate to join with 194 other nations in ratifying the United Nations Convention on the Rights of the Child.

A 2019 resolution on the general issue of global forced migration was considered and approved by both churches. In that resolution, the specific rights of Palestinian refugees under United Nations Security Council 194 (1948) were affirmed, which states that "refugees wishing to return to their homes and live at peace with their neighbours should be permitted to do so at the earliest practicable date, and that compensation should be paid for the property of those choosing not to return and for loss of or damage to property." The resolution also called for the U.S. to continue to support the United Nations Relief and Works Agency, which was established in 1949 to address the needs of Palestine refugees.

A significant shift took place in response to the Kairos Palestine "Cry for Hope," issued in July 2020. The "Cry for Hope" letter called on "all Christians and on churches at congregational, denominational, national, and global ecumenical levels to engage in a process of study, reflection and confession concerning the historic and systemic deprivation of the rights of the Palestinian people, and the use of the Bible by many to justify and support this oppression." This call was taken seriously, and the two churches adopted resolutions—with overwhelming margins—at their next Synod and Assembly in direct response to these Palestinian Christian voices.

In 2021 the UCC General Synod adopted a "Declaration for a Just Peace between Palestine and Israel," and in 2023 the Disciples General Assembly passed "Compelled to Witness." The resolutions were parallel and marked a watershed moment in that the policies the resolutions contained moved the churches away from a proscriptive approach (focusing on a particular outcome such as a two-state solution), toward a rights-based approach. The parallel resolutions named Israel's system of laws and legal procedures as apartheid, called the oppression of the Palestinian people a matter of theological urgency and a sin in violation of scripture, rejected the notion that criticism of Israeli policies and practices is inherently antisemitic, and rejected any theology, including Christian Zionism, that privileges or excludes one group of people to another. They also named (again for the UCC) the churches' affirmation of the right to employ economic measures to support justice, a right grounded in the First Amendment of the U.S. Constitution. These resolutions called for the cessation of U.S. military aid to Israel and called for the U.S. to restore full funding for the United Nations Relief and Works Agency.

It is noteworthy that the UCC and the Disciples were the first and third denominations to name the apartheid framework to describe the reality in Israel/Palestine. The moral and theological voice of the churches was clear in the naming of the oppression of the Palestinian people as sin.

UCC and Disciples members, in considering such resolutions, have expressed awareness of the potential impact on interfaith relations. Both churches are deeply engaged in interfaith dialogue and have policies that support such engagement as well as opposing antisemitism and anti-Muslim attitudes and actions. The UCC in 1987 adopted a resolution affirming its relationships with the Jewish community, and the Disciples in 1993 considered and approved a "Statement on Relations Between Jews and Christians." Both churches noted the historical relations of our faiths, and denounced antisemitism. The UCC further passed a resolution on antisemitism in 2001. In 1989 the UCC adopted a resolution on its relationship with the Muslim community, and in 2011 both churches passed parallel resolutions on actions of hostility against Islam and the Muslim community.

In addition to General Synod and General Assembly resolutions, UCC and Disciples leadership regularly issue statements and pastoral letters on issues of concern to the church. Numerous such statements and pastoral letters have been published by the two churches' General Ministers and Presidents, officers and ministry heads, and/or Co-Executives of Global Ministries. While too many to recount in this space, it is perhaps particularly relevant to draw attention to the UCC Executive Leaders' statement, "A Prophetic Call for Justice and Peace in Palestine" ((July 24, 2024), and "A pastoral letter for peace and justice from leaders of the Christian Church (Disciples of Christ)" (Sept. 3, 2024). Both letters were issued in the midst of Israel's ongoing war on the Palestinians, and both named Israel's campaign as genocide. The UCC leaders' letter set the current war in the context of other atrocities in the world, and called for its end, for root causes to be addressed, and for accountability, as well as naming Christian complicity through theologies "which justify violence, emphasize superiority, privilege, and supremacy, and support harmful colonial acts." The Disciples leaders stated, for their part, "We must name injustice when we see it, and also act to re-center our Christian values of peace with justice, compassion, and love for all people – the weak as well as the strong, the poor as well as the wealthy, and the powerless as well as the powerful. We cannot succumb to the sin of apathy but must speak truth to power with clarity and with prayer, wisdom, and action."

Over the course of these decades the positions of the churches have responded both to the times and to the calls of partners. As our understanding of mission continues to emphasize accompaniment and mutuality, and as that understanding spreads through our churches, the policies and positions adopted by General Assembly and General Synod have continued to evolve to reflect the desire of our churches to offer meaningful solidarity with partners near and far and support the quest for a just peace in the Middle East.

DISCUSSION QUESTIONS

1. Since the current incarnations of our two denominations, we have focused on the need for peace and demilitarization in the Middle East broadly and in Israel/Palestine specifically. Why is it important for us as churches to state that in our policies?

2. More recently, our two churches have spoken up against the ongoing Israeli occupation. What effect do you think that has had on your local church and for our partners in the region?

3. Why is it important that our churches' policies are informed by our global partners, mission personnel, and members of our churches?

4. What might you do to engage your local congregation in understanding these resolutions? Could understanding and promoting the resolutions help deepen your congregation's commitment to supporting Palestinian siblings?

Appendix B

2021 UCC General Synod Resolution Declaration For a Just Peace Between Palestine and Israel

WHEREAS for over seventy years Palestinian people have faced dispossession of their land, displacement from their homes, a harsh military occupation, severe restrictions on travel, the military detention of their children, home demolitions—over 120,000 to date and the constant threat of more—and vast inequities in access to natural, economic, and medical resources when compared to that enjoyed by Israeli citizens living in illegal West Bank settlements, and also on a daily basis face severe restrictions on access to their olive groves, farms, and holy sites; and

WHEREAS there are more than 5.6 million Palestinian refugees registered with the United Nations Relief and Works Administration representing a global displacement of Palestinian people dating back to 1948 whose future status remains unresolved; and

WHEREAS the Israeli government has maintained an illegal military occupation of Palestinian territories since 1967 that includes the establishment of illegal Jewish-only settlements throughout the West Bank and more recently has enacted formal discrimination against its Arab citizens through the passage of the Nation State Law in 2018; and

WHEREAS provocative actions under the Trump administration, including moving the U.S. embassy to Jerusalem, the suspension of humanitarian aid to the United Nations Relief and Works Administration [*sic*], and support for Israel's proposed illegal annexation of land in the occupied West Bank have further injured the Palestinian community and imposed serious road blocks to peace; and

WHEREAS the Trump Administration's Department of Education has issued a rule labeling any criticism of the State of Israel as an antisemitic act in order to suppress advocacy for Palestinian rights on university campuses, and has joined many state governments in further suppressing freedom of speech in support of Palestinian civil society's call for boycotts, divestment, and sanctions; and

WHEREAS actions by Israel, with tacit and overt support from the United States government, have established conditions comparable to those in force under Jim Crow in the United States south between Reconstruction and the Civil Rights Movement, with segregation laws that enshrined systematic domination and oppression by whites over blacks. Israel's acts of domination and oppression include, but are not limited to adoption of the Nation State Law in 2018, the building of the separation barrier, implementation of a restrictive pass system for Palestinians, the creation of Israeli-only highways through the West Bank, and imposed military detention of Palestinian children accused of crimes; and

WHEREAS the General Synod of the United Church of Christ and its officers have for over fifty years advocated for a negotiated process leading to a just peace between Israel and Palestine marked by adherence to international law and international standards of human rights and honoring the principle of self-determination and the rights of Palestinian refugees; and

WHEREAS, reminiscent of historical examples such as the United States, Canada, Australia, and Southern Africa, Israel exhibits a current-day form of settler colonialism, actively engaged in the removal and erasure of the indigenous Palestinian population, through a matrix of control that includes: the imposition of a harsh military occupation; the de facto annexation of Palestinian lands and threats of further annexation; the expansion of illegal Jewish only settlements in East Jerusalem and the West Bank; the contraction of Palestinian-controlled land; and the restriction of travel for Palestinians in the West Bank and Gaza;

WHEREAS *Cry for Hope: A Call for Decisive Action* issued by Palestinian Christian leaders and theologians in July 2020 states that "the very being of the church, the integrity of the Christian faith, and the credibility of the Gospel is at stake. We declare that support for the oppression of the Palestinian people, whether passive or active, through silence, word or deed, is a sin. We assert that Christian support for Zionism as a theology and an ideology that legitimize the right of one people to deny the human rights of another is incompatible with the Christian faith and a grave misuse of the Bible";

THEREFORE, BE IT RESOLVED that the Thirty-Third General Synod of the United Church of Christ adopts the following Declaration:

1. *We affirm* that the continued oppression of the Palestinian people remains, after more than five decades of oppression of the Palestinian people, a matter of theological urgency and represents a sin in violation of the message of the biblical prophets and the Gospel, and that all efforts to defend or legitimate the oppression of the Palestinian people, whether passive or active, through silence, word, or deed by the Christian community, represent a fundamental denial of the Gospel.

   Therefore, we reject the notion that Israel's occupation of Palestine is a purely political problem outside the concern of the church or that the oppression of the Palestinian people is an inevitable consequence of global or regional geopolitical interests.

2. *We affirm* that the biblical narrative beginning with creation and extending through the calling of the Israelites, the corrective admonitions of the prophets, the incarnation and ministry of Jesus and the witness of the apostles to the "ends of the earth" ... speaks of God's blessing extending to "all the families of the earth." (Genesis 12.3)

   Therefore, we reject any theology or ideology including Christian Zionism, Supercessionism, antisemitism or anti-Islam bias that would privilege or exclude any one nation, race, culture, or religion within God's universal economy of grace.

3. *We affirm* that all people living in Palestine and Israel are created in the image of God and that this bestows ultimate dignity and sacredness to all;

    Therefore, we reject any laws and legal procedures which are used by one race or religion or political entity to enshrine one people in a privileged legal position at the expense of another, including Israel's apartheid system of laws and legal procedures.

4. *We affirm* that all peoples have the right to self-determination and to their aspirations for sovereignty and statehood in the shaping of their corporate religious, cultural, and political life, free from manipulation or pressure from outside powers, and that a just resolution of conflicting claims is only achieved through the equal protection of civil rights, the fair and just sharing of land and resources, and peaceful negotiation based on international law and UN resolutions.

    Therefore, we reject the use of Scripture to claim a divine right to the land as the rationale for Israel's illegal seizure and annexation of Palestinian land as well as the imposition of so-called peace agreements by Israel or the United States through the exercise of political and military domination that leaves Palestinians without equal rights, full citizenship, and the opportunity to thrive religiously, culturally, politically, and economically.

5. *We affirm* the rights of Palestinian refugees to return to their homes if they so choose or to be compensated for their loss of property, consistent with UN General Assembly resolution 194 (1948).

    Therefore, we reject the denial of this right, just as we reject efforts to manipulate internationally-agreed upon definitions of refugees to attempt to erase this right which extends across generations.

6. *We affirm* the First Amendment constitutional right to freedom of speech and assembly to protest the actions of the State of

Israel and to uphold the rights of Palestinians, including the use of economic measures to support justice as a First Amendment right and joining the international Boycott, Divestment, and Sanctions movement by individuals, institutions, corporations, and religious bodies that advocate peace with justice or participate in any aspect of the use of economic measures to support justice.

Therefore, we reject the idea that any criticism of policies of the State of Israel is inherently antisemitic, in confession that some criticism is antisemitic in intent or impact, and we oppose the efforts of U.S. federal and state governments to limit free speech on university campuses and to restrict or ban support of the international Boycott, Divestment, and Sanctions movement.

BE IT FURTHER RESOLVED that national setting of the United Church of Christ send the text of this Declaration to Local Churches, Associations and Conferences; and

BE IT FINALLY RESOLVED that all settings of the United Church of Christ be encouraged to receive this Declaration as a prophetic call for renewed and continued advocacy for a just peace in Palestine and Israel and use it as a plumbline for taking action, including, for example:

a. Committing to hearing the voices of Palestinians regarding their situation, including the voices of Palestinian Christians through the study of Palestine Liberation Theology, attention to statements and appeals such as Kairos Palestine: A Moment of Truth (2009) and a Cry for Hope (2020), participation in travel seminars that expose visitors to the Palestinian community, and use of resources from Global Ministries of the United Church of Christ and the Christian Church (Disciples of Christ).

b. Implementing the calls of prior General Synod resolutions, including the 2015 Resolution, "A Call for the United Church of Christ to Take Actions Toward a Just Peace in the Israeli-Palestinian Conflict," and the 2017 Resolution,

"A Call for the United Church of Christ to Advocate for the Rights of Children Living Under Israeli Military Occupation."

c.   Examining critically our use and interpretations of Scripture as well as liturgies and hymns that equate ancient Biblical Israel with the modern state in ways that promote settler colonialism and the dispossession of Palestinian land, rights, and cultural expressions.

d.   Offering support and encouragement to college students and faculty members as well as the human rights groups (including Students for Justice in Palestine, Jewish Voice for Peace, American Muslims for Palestine, and many other allied groups), whose freedom to speak, witness and advocate on university campuses is threatened in any way by state or local governments, or by college administrators.

e.   Advocating for the cessation of U.S. military aid to Israel until such time that Palestinian human rights, civil rights, and self-determination are fully realized and protected in compliance with international law, US laws on foreign military assistance, and the principles of human rights.

f.   Supporting the full restoration of US funding for the United Nations Relief and Works Agency which carries out critical services by and for Palestinian refugees, and encouraging continued support for UCC partners which serve Palestinian refugees.

g.   Demanding that the plight of Palestinian refugees be addressed by Israel and the international community based on United Nations Resolution 194 guaranteeing that "refugees wishing to return to their homes and live at peace with their neighbours should be permitted to do so at the earliest practicable date, and that compensation should be paid for the property of those choosing not to return and for loss of or damage to property which, under principles of international law or equity, should be made good by the Governments or authorities responsible."

Appendix C

2023 Disciples General Assembly Resolution

Compelled To Witness: Answering The Cry of Our Palestinian Siblings

WHEREAS the Christian Church (Disciples of Christ) in the United States and Canada sent its first missionary to Palestine in 1851 and, through more than a dozen Christian Church (Disciples of Christ) mission partners in Israel and Palestine, Disciples have worked alongside the people there with appointed mission workers and financial support; and

WHEREAS the Christian Church (Disciples of Christ) has a history of commitment to racial, economic and social justice; and has spoken clearly and participated actively in movements for civil rights and anti-racism in the US and Canada and for human rights and the just resolution of conflict around the world; and between 1973 and 2019, our General Assembly has articulated clear positions in support of justice and peace for Palestinians and Israelis; and

WHEREAS the establishment of the State of Israel led to the 75-year displacement and dispossession of hundreds of thousands of Palestinians from their homes and property—amounting to a modern-day form of settler colonialism and creating a refugee population that now numbers more than 7 million; and the State of Israel has imposed a harsh 56-years-long occupation of East Jerusalem, the West Bank and Gaza Strip; and

WHEREAS globally recognized human rights organizations—including B'Tselem-The Israeli Information Center for Human Rights in the Occupied Territories, Human Rights Watch, and Amnesty International—and the United Nations' Special Rapporteur have issued detailed reports describing the State of Israel's apartheid system; and

WHEREAS in February 2022, Disciples leaders issued a Pastoral Letter, Compelled to Witness: Affirming Justice, Rights, and Accountability in Promoting Peace in Israel/Palestine, naming actions and circumstances that have led to the deterioration of hope for a just peace in Israel/Palestine, and finding that "Israeli policies and practices that discriminate against Palestinians—Christian and Muslims alike—are consistent with the international legal definition of the crime of apartheid as defined in the International Convention on the Suppression and Punishment of the Crime of Apartheid (ICSPCA, 1973) and the Rome Statute of the International Criminal Court (2002)"; and

WHEREAS a just and lasting peace between Israel and Palestine must be grounded in the message of Scripture, both in the Hebrew prophets and the life and teachings of Jesus, as well as international law and globally recognized human rights conventions; and

WHEREAS in December 2009, our mission partner Kairos Palestine issued *A Moment of Truth: A word of faith, hope, and love from the heart of Palestinian Suffering*, a profoundly theological document grounded in the Biblical texts, which declares:

> ... We believe that our land has a universal mission. In this universality, the meaning of the promises, of the land, of the election, of the people of God open up to include all of humanity, starting from all the peoples of this land. In light of the teachings of the Holy Bible, the promise of the land has never been a political programme, but rather the prelude to complete universal salvation. It was the initiation of the fulfilment of the Kingdom of God on earth (KP 2.3); and

WHEREAS *Cry for Hope: A Call for Decisive Action*, issued in July 2020 by Palestinian Christian leaders and theologians, states that "the very being of the church, the integrity of the Christian faith, and the credibility of the Gospel is at stake," and "support for the oppression of the Palestinian people, whether passive or active, through silence, word or deed, is a sin"; and

WHEREAS in 2022, Kairos Palestine published A Dossier on Israeli Apartheid: A Pressing Call to Churches Around the World, a resource that: points to the conditions necessary to establish the crime of apartheid; offers a Biblical/theological reflection that describes the sin of apartheid; reminds readers that "The church has named and resisted the sin and injustice of apartheid in the past"; and repeats the Palestinians' cry, "Are you able to help us get our freedom back, for this is the only way you can help the two peoples attain justice, peace, security and love?";

THEREFORE, BE IT RESOLVED that the General Assembly of the Christian Church (Disciples of Christ) in the United States and Canada, meeting in Louisville, Kentucky, July 29-August 1, 2023:

- Embraces an understanding that the Bible's narrative—beginning with creation and extending through the calling of the Israelites, the prophets' witness, the ministry of Jesus, the witness of the apostles, and Revelation's vision of a new heaven and a new earth and the Tree of Life, the leaves of which are for the healing of the nations—speaks of God's blessing extending to "all the families of the earth (Genesis 12.3)"; and

- Believes that all people living in Palestine and Israel are created in the image of God deserving of equal dignity and their human rights; and

- Affirms the 2022 Disciples leadership Pastoral Letter, Compelled to Witness: Affirming Justice, Rights, and Accountability in Promoting Peace in Israel/Palestine; and

- Asserts that the continued oppression of the Palestinian people is a matter of theological urgency and represents a sin in violation of the message of the Biblical prophets and the Gospel, and that all efforts to defend or legitimate the oppression of the Palestinian people represent a fundamental denial of the Gospel; and

- Rejects any theology or ideology including Christian Zionism, supercessionism, antisemitism or anti-Islam bias that would privilege or exclude any one nation, race, culture, or religion; and

- Condemns speech and acts of antisemitism, and rejects the notion that criticism of policies of the State of Israel is inherently antisemitic; and

BE IT FURTHER RESOLVED that the General Assembly:

- Affirms that many of the laws, policies and practices of the State of Israel meet the definition of apartheid as defined in international law, documented in the reports cited above, and described as such by some of our mission partners over the past two decades, and affirmed in our Disciples leaders' pastoral letter, Compelled to Witness; and

- Affirms that all peoples have the right to self-determination and to their aspirations for full and equal citizenship in the shaping of their corporate religious, cultural, and political life, and that a just resolution of conflicting claims is only achieved through the equal protection of civil and human rights, the fair and just sharing of land and resources, and peaceful negotiation based on international law and UN resolutions; and

- Calls for an end to Israel's occupation of the Palestinian territories consistent with international law and UN resolutions; and

- Affirms the rights of Palestinian refugees to return to their homes if they so choose or to be compensated for their loss of property, consistent with UN General Assembly resolution 194; and

- Insists on the U.S. constitutional right to freedom of speech and assembly to protest the laws, policies and practices of the State of Israel and to support the rights of Palestinians, including the use of economic measures by individuals, institutions, corporations and religious bodies that advocate for lasting peace with justice; and

FINALLY, BE IT FURTHER RESOLVED that congregations, regions, general units and related institutions and organizations of the Christian Church (Disciples of Christ) be encouraged to:

- Listen to the voices of Palestinians, with special attention to statements such as *Kairos Palestine: A Moment of Truth* (2009) and *Cry for Hope* (2020), and;

- Participate in travel opportunities that expose pilgrims to the Palestinian community; and

- Make use of resources from Global Ministries of the Christian Church (Disciples of Christ) and the United Church of Christ; and

- Use this resolution to guide their support for the aspirations of our denominational partners in the region and in our advocacy with the governments of the United States and Canada consistent with the call in Compelled to Witness.

Further Reading

General

- Global Ministries. "Resources on the Middle East." https://www.globalministries.org/resource/mee_resources_index/.
- The Israel Committee Against House Demolitions, founded by Jeff Halper, provides information about the "matrix of control" along with other valuable resources on its website, www.icahd.org.
- Khalidi, Rashid. *The Hundred Years War on Palestine*. New York: Picador, 2020.
- Roy, Sara. *The Gaza Strip: The Political Economy of De-development*. Beirut: Institute for Palestine Studies, 1995.
- Thrall, Nathan. *A Day in the Life of Abed Salama*. New York: Metropolitan Books, 2023.
- Tolan, Sandy. *The Lemon Tree*. New York: Bloomsbury Publishing, 2006.
- Zaru, Jean. *Occupied with Nonviolence: A Palestinian Woman Speaks*. Fortress Press, 2008.

Contributors' Publications

- Ateek, Naim. *A Palestinian Christian Cry for Reconciliation*. Orbis Books, 2008.
- Ateek, Naim. *A Palestinian Theology of Liberation: The Bible, Justice, and the Palestine-Israel Conflict*. Orbis Books, 2017.
- Ateek, Naim. *Call and Commitment: A Journey of Faith From Nakba to Palestinian Liberation Theology*. Eugene, OR: Cascade Books, 2023.
- Ateek, Naim. *Justice and Only Justice*. Orbis Books, 1989.
- Isaac, Munther. *The Other Side of the Wall: A Palestinian Christian Narrative of Lament and Hope*. IVP, 2020.

- Kassis, Rifat Odeh. *Kairos for Palestine*. Badayl/Alternatives, 2011.
- Kuttab, Johnathan. *Beyond the Two-State Solution*. 2022. www.nonviolenceinternational.net/beyond2states.
- Raheb, Mitri. *Bethlehem Besieged*. Fortress Press, 2004.
- Raheb, Mitri. *Decolonizing Palestine: The Land, the People, the Bible*. Orbis Books, 2023.
- Raheb, Mitri. *Faith in the Face of Empire*. Orbis Books, 2014.
- Raheb, Mitri. *I Am a Palestinian Christian*. Fortress Press, 1995.
- Sabella, Bernard. *A Life Worth Living: The Story of a Palestinian Catholic*. Resource Publications, an Imprint of Wipf and Stock Publishers, 2018.

Christian Zionism Resources

- ChristianZionism.org, https://www.christianzionism.org/.
- Koshy, Ninan. "Christian Zionism." Global Ministries. https://www.globalministries.org/mee_resources_christian_zionism_koshy/.
- Middle East Council of Churches. *What is Western Fundamentalist Christian Zionism?* Global Ministries. 1988. https://www.globalministries.org/wp-content/uploads/nb/pages/6781/attachments/original/1578600352/MECC_Christian_Zionism.pdf?1578600352.
- Polley, Gabriel. "Jerusalem through Evangelical Eyes: Nineteenth-Century Western Encounters with Palestinian Christianity." *Jerusalem Quarterly* (Summer 2021). https://www.palestine-studies.org/sites/default/files/jq-articles/Jerusalem%20through%20Evangelical%20Eyes.pdf.
- Smith, Robert O. *More Desired than Our Owne Salvation: The Roots of Christian Zionism*. Oxford University Press, 2013.

Apartheid Resources

- Apartheid-Free Campaign, https://apartheid-free.org/pledge/.

- Amnesty International. "Israel's Apartheid Against Palestinians: Cruel System of Domination and Crime Against Humanity." February 1, 2022. https://www.amnesty.org/en/documents/mde15/5141/2022/en/.

- B'Tselem. "A Regime of Jewish Supremacy from the Jordan River to the Mediterranean Sea: This Is Apartheid." January 12, 2021. https://www.btselem.org/publications/fulltext/202101_this_is_apartheid.

- B'Tselem. "Not a Vibrant Democracy. This Is Apartheid." 2022. https://www.btselem.org/publications/202210_not_a_vibrant_democracy_this_is_apartheid.

- Human Rights Watch. "A Threshold Crossed." April 27, 2021. https://www.hrw.org/report/2021/04/27/threshold-crossed/israeli-authorities-and-crimes-apartheid-and-persecution.

- Kairos Palestine. "A Moment of Truth." 2009. https://kairospalestine.ps/index.php/about-kairos/kairos-palestine-document.

- Kairos Palestine. "Cry For Hope." July 1, 2020. https://cryforhope.org/media/attachments/2020/06/30/cry-for-hope-english.pdf.

- Sabeel Ecumenical Liberation Theology Center. "The Apartheid Paradigm." *Cornerstone* 48 (2008). https://sabeel.org/wp-content/uploads/2016/03/CornerstoneIssue48.pdf.

Contributors

Rev. Dr. Naim Stifan Ateek, an Anglican priest, is a Palestinian Arab and a citizen of Israel. A former canon of St. George's Cathedral, Jerusalem, he is founder of Sabeel, an ecumenical center in Jerusalem that uses a theological approach to work for liberation for Palestinians. He is the author of *Justice and Only Justice* and *A Palestinian Christian Cry for Reconciliation*.

Rev. Dr. LaMarco Antonio Cable serves as the President of Disciples Overseas Ministries and Co-Executive of Global Ministries of the Christian Church (Disciples of Christ) and United Church of Christ. Hailing from Memphis, Tennessee, he is a pastor, preacher, advocate, and community organizer deeply rooted in his faith and commitment to social justice. His prior service within Global Ministries includes roles such as Area Executive for Africa, Advocacy Associate, and Interim Mission Personnel Executive. In addition to serving congregations in Tennessee, Kentucky, and the District of Columbia, Cable also served as Deputy Director for Organizing at Bread for the World. Cable also serves on Lexington Theological Seminary's Alumni Council and the National City Christian Church Foundation.

Rebekah Choate has served since 2017 as Minister for Global Advocacy and Education for Global Ministries of the Christian Church (Disciples of Christ) and United Church of Christ. Prior to this call she worked for an international educational exchange nonprofit organization. Born and raised in a UCC church in a small city in Maine with an international relations academic background, she firmly believes in the transformative power of visiting new places and learning from people from other communities and cultures.

Derek Duncan is the Global Relations Minister for East Asia and the Pacific for Global Ministries of the Christian Church (Disciples of Christ) and the United Church of Christ. In this position he accompanies partner churches and institutions from China to the Pacific islands in areas of mutual church mission and program support, ecumenical cooperation, development and disaster assistance, and advocacy. Previously Duncan served Global Ministries as Associate for Global Advocacy and Education and NGO representative to the United Nations, focusing on East Asia, Southern Asia, the Middle East, and Europe, as well as issues of climate change, economic justice, and interfaith understanding.

Rev. Dr. Munther Isaac is a Palestinian Christian pastor and theologian. He currently pastors the Evangelical Lutheran Christmas Church in Bethlehem and the Lutheran Church in Beit Sahour. He is also the Academic Dean of Bethlehem Bible College and Director of the Christ at the Checkpoint conferences. He speaks locally and internationally and has published numerous articles on issues related to the theology of the land, Palestinian Christians and Palestinian theology, holistic mission, and reconciliation. He is the author of several books on Palestine, Palestinian theology, biblical commentary, and the ordination of women. He is also involved in many reconciliation and interfaith forums. He is a Kairos Palestine board member.

Rifat Kassis has over thirty-five years of experience in human rights, mainly child rights, working in the Middle East, Northern Caucasus, Central Asia, and Europe. He founded the Palestinian section of the global child rights movement, Defense for Children International, co-founded its movement in the Arab World, and was elected International President for two terms in Geneva. He was also selected to be the State of Palestine candidate for the UN Committee on the Rights of the Child. He cofounded the Alternative Tourism Group, Occupied Palestine and Global Heights Advocacy Initiative, and The National Coalition of Christian Organizations. He founded the YMCA/YWCA Olive Tree Campaign. He is one of the co-authors of Kairos Palestine document and its General Coordinator as well as its global coalition.

Jonathan Kuttab is Executive Director of Friends of Sabeel North America. In addition to being a cofounder of Sabeel, Jerusalem, Kuttab is a cofounder of the Palestinian human rights group Al-Haq and cofounder of Nonviolence International. A well-known international human rights attorney, Kuttab practices in the United States, Palestine, and Israel. He serves on the board of Bethlehem Bible College and is President of the Board of Holy Land Trust. Jonathan was the head of the Legal Committee negotiating the Cairo Agreement of 1994 between Israel and the Palestinian Liberation Organization. After graduating from the University of Virginia Law School and practicing on Wall Street, Jonathan returned home to Palestine and East Jerusalem. He is a partner of Kuttab, Khoury, and Hanna Law Firm in East Jerusalem.

Krista Johnson Weicksel serves as the Vice President for Administration and Programs for Disciples Overseas Ministries. She first served with Global Ministries as a Global Mission Intern in Jerusalem with Sabeel Ecumenical Liberation Theology Center. She went on to serve as the International Peacebuilding Coordinator for Mennonite Central Committee and the Global Advocacy and Education Associate for Global Ministries. Johnson Weicksel is a lifelong Disciple and serves on several boards in the life of the Christian Church (Disciples of Christ). Johnson Weicksel's academic background is in peacebuilding and conflict resolution. She is a Strategies for Trauma Awareness and Resilience trainer and a Society for Human Resource Management Certified Professional.

Dr. Peter E. Makari serves as Global Relations Minister for the Middle East and Europe with Global Ministries, a position he has held since 2000. He serves as a co-convener of the National Council of Churches' Interreligious Convening Table and has participated in national Jewish-Christian and Muslim-Christian dialogue initiatives. He represents the United Church of Christ and Disciples on the Faith Forum for Middle East Policy as a co-convener and on the board of Churches for Middle East Peace. An Egyptian-American, Dr. Makari has lived in the Middle East, where he worked with the Coptic Evangelical Organization for Social Services in Cairo, Egypt, and the Middle East Council of Churches, based in Cyprus.

Rev. Shari Prestemon began her service as Acting Associate General Minister and Co-Executive of Global Ministries in January 2024, following a career in congregational, denominational, and nonprofit ministry. Prestemon's faith journey has been profoundly shaped by direct experiences with the ministries she now supports in her current role with Global Ministries. She served as a Peace and Justice Intern for one year in the Philippines and led multiple study trips to Palestine and Israel, Haiti, Columbia, Germany, Indonesia, and East Timor. She partnered extensively with Global H.O.P.E. when Hurricane Katrina devastated Back Bay Mission and the Gulf Coast region in 2005.

Rev. Prof. Mitri Raheb is Founder and President of Dar al-Kalima University in Bethlehem. The most widely published Palestinian theologian to date, Dr. Raheb is the author and editor of fifty books. Rev. Raheb served as Senior Pastor of the Christmas Lutheran Church in Bethlehem for three decades and as President of the Synod of the Evangelical Lutheran Church in Jordan and the Holy Land from 2011–2016. A social entrepreneur, Rev. Raheb has founded several NGOs, including the Christian Academic Forum for Citizenship in the Arab World. He is a founding and board member of the National Library of Palestine and a founding member of Bright Stars of Bethlehem.

Dr. Mira Rizeq is President of the World YWCA. She is a recognized leader with over thirty-five years of solid local, regional, and international experience in development work as well as a strong advocate for women's rights and justice, including social, political, and economic justice globally. Rizeq worked in several local and international NGOs, including UNDP in Palestine and as former General Secretary of the YWCA of Palestine. She has worked for several international organizations focused on Palestine. An activist in human rights, especially women's rights, Mira has served on several boards of women's institutions and acted as an advisor to several UN agencies especially on women's empowerment strategies.

Dr. Bernard Sabella was born in Jerusalem in 1945. He studied at the Freres School, New Gate Jerusalem, and went on to study at Franklin and Marshall College in Lancaster, Pennsylvania, and onward to the University of Virginia, where he earned both M.A. and Ph.D. degrees in sociology. He taught for twenty-five years at Bethlehem University and later joined the Department of Service to Palestinian Refugees of the Middle East Council of Churches as its Director. His research interests focus on Palestinian Christians and immigration. He is now retired but continues to follow up on his research interests, including interreligious relations in Palestine and across the Middle East.